State of the World's Street Children: **Violence**

Sarah Thomas de Benítez

Street Children Series

First published in Great Britain in 2007 by
Consortium for Street Children (UK)
Unit 306, Bon Marche Centre
241-251 Ferndale Road
LONDON
SW9 8BJ

ISBN: 978-0-9547886-5-0

State of the World's Street Children: Violence report is available for download from the Consortium for Street Children website (www.streetchildren.org.uk). A hardcopy can be ordered by contacting the Consortium for Street Children by e-mail (info@streetchildren.org.uk).

Cover Design
Annabel Clements

Cover Photographer
Pep Bonet (Caption: Young boys photographed on the streets of Freetown, Sierra Leone)

Report Design
The Policy Press (www.policypress.org.uk)

Printed in the UK by
Latimer Trend, Plymouth

Special thanks to Neide Cassaniga for the main literature review for this report and to Anita Schrader McMillan as co-author of Chapter 3 and for a wealth of additional academic references.

Parts of this publication may be copied for use in research, advocacy and education, providing the source is acknowledged. This publication may not be reproduced for other purposes without the prior permission of the Consortium for Street Children.

Acknowledgements

Principal Author
Sarah Thomas de Benítez

Project Manager
Christian Harris

Expert Task Force Members
Nicola Brewer, Chief Executive, Commission for Equality and Human Rights, UK
Neide Cassaniga, Independent Researcher on Street Children
Gareth A. Jones, Department of Geography, London School of Economics and Political Science
Marcus Lyon, Photographer
Anita Schrader McMillan, Warwick Medical School and former Director of the Consortium for Street Children

Violence Working Group Members
Emily Bild (Plan UK), Sarah Burt (Street Child Africa), Alex Dressler (CSC), Cassie Hague (CSC), Jonathan Hannay (ACER), Felix Holman (Street Child Africa), Lisa James (Plan), Pete Kent (Railway Children), Philippa Loates (ICT), David Maidment, Carile Marchioro (CSC), Ali Monodee (ABC Trust), Angela Murray (Toybox), Helen Nash (Toybox), Marta Persiani (ChildHope), Sheila Royce (Casa Alianza), Anita Schraeder, Liz Trippett (EveryChild)

Case Studies Contributed by
Catherine Klirodotakou and Marta Persiani (ChildHope); Maggie Eno (M'Lop Tapang) and Philippa Loates (International Childcare Trust); Sanat Kumar Sinha (Bal Sakha); Sylvia Reyes (JUCONI Ecuador); Gisella Hanley (Viva a Vida); Andy Sexton (180° Alliance) and Angela Murray (Toybox); Miguel Angel López (CONACMI) and Anita Schrader McMillan (Warwick Medical School); Catholic Action for Street Children, Street Child Nigeria – The Daughters of Charity, The Rainbow Project – Association Pope John XXIII, and Streets Ahead with Street Child Africa; Ahmed Shaaban, Sandra Azmy, Huessien Hassan, Reda Haggag and Jacinthe Ibrahim (Plan Egypt) with Andrew Stephens; Gulnara Asylbekova and Ainura Tekenova (EveryChild Kyrgyzstan); Alison Lane (JUCONI Mexico); Kate McAlpine (Mkombozi); Maria Jose Meza and Maria del Mar Murillo (World Vision International, Latin American & Caribbean Regional Office); Amy Price (War Child); Chandini Tilakaratna (Shilpa Children's Trust) and Philippa Loates (International Childcare Trust)

Country Papers Provided by
Antoinette Amuzu, Cristian Badiu, Max Baldwin, Sarah Boardman, Catherine Bunten, Jessica Cadesky, Njeri Chege, Grace Choong, Claire Louise Cody, Katie Dimmer, Emma Fanning, Guillem Fortuny Fillo, Jessica Greenhalf, Ana Guerreiro, Sharon Horder, Celina Jensen, Jonathan Kennedy, Amanda Lee, Sarah Lloyd, Bárbara Magalhães, Kathryn Mahoney, Valerie Marechal, Rebecca Morton, Sophie Oliver, Jackie Otunnu, Jennifer Pido, Laurent Pompanon, Rebecca Procope, Lily Rahnema, Federica Riccardi, Clara Rodríguez Ribas, Solène Rougeaux, Pratima Sood, Pudthila Srisontisuk, Andrew Stephens, Marta Valsecchi, Elena Walsh, Anna de Courcy Wheeler

Photography by
Pep Bonet, Donna DeCesare, Robin Hammond, Marcus Lyon, Dario Mitidieri, Karen Robinson and Dieter Telemans. Special thanks to Panos (www.panos.co.uk) for the use of photos by Pep Bonet, Karen Robinson and Dieter Telemans

Report Reviewed by
Assefa Bequele (The African Child Policy Forum), Anees Jillani (SPARC), Dwight Ordóñez, Emilie Smeaton (Railway Children) and Svetlana Stephenson (London Metropolitan University).

Input also received from
Sandra Brobbey (Plan), Emily Browne (CSC), Rosemary Camperos (CSC), Emma Crewe (ChildHope), Trudy Davies, James Georgalakis (EveryChild), Jessica Muir (CSC), Surina Narula, Ruth Payne, David Williams, Fred Shortland (Casa Alianza), Christian Wolmer

With special thanks to the children and staff from across the world who shared their perceptions and materials for use in this report.

Table of Contents

Acknowledgements — iii
Foreword — vi
Executive Summary — vii
Introduction — 1

Chapter 1 Violence and Street Children: An Ecological Model — 6

Chapter 2 Street Children as Individuals: Young Lives and Violence — 8
  Recommendations: Street Children as Individuals — 15

Chapter 3 Street Children and Relationships: Violence in the Home — 16
(Co-authored by Anita Schrader)
  Recommendations: Street Children and Family Violence — 22

Chapter 4 Street Children and Violence in the Community — 24
  Street Children and Violence in the Home Neighbourhood — 24
  Recommendations: Street Children and the Neighbourhood Community — 30
  Street Children and Violence in the Street — 31
  Recommendations on Street Children and Violence in Public Spaces — 41

Chapter 5 Street Children and Violence in Society — 42
  Street Children and Violence in Residential Facilities — 42
  Recommendations on Street Children and Violence in Institutions — 47
  Street Children and Violence in Wider Society — 47
  Recommendations on Street Children and Violence in Society — 57

Chapter 6 Conclusion: Street Children and Violence — 58

Chapter 7 Street Children and Violence: Statistics and Methodology — 64
  Street Children and Statistics: An Introduction — 64
  Methodological Difficulties in Producing Statistics about Street Children — 64
  Societies, Street Children and Violence: Moving Towards Statistical Analysis — 67
  Recommendations for Research — 69
  A Statistical Table: Societies, Street Children and Violence — 71

References **82**
Case Study Footnotes **91**
About the Photographers **93**

Figures
1	A Typology of Violence	3
2	Ecological Model for Understanding Risk and Protective Factors of Violence	7

Case Studies
1	Street Children in Bangladesh	9
2	Street Children in Cambodia	12
3	Street Children and Family Violence in India	17
4	Street Children and Reconciliation in Sierra Leone	20
5	Street Children and Community Schools in Ecuador	25
6	Street Children and Drugs in Salvador, Brazil	28
7	Street Children and State-sponsored Police Violence in Uganda	32
8	Street Children and Police in Guatemala	34
9	Street Children and Violence in African Streets	36
10	Street Children and Public Stigmatization: Egypt	38
11	Street Children and Detention in Kyrgyzstan	43
12	Street Children and Protection in Care in Mexico	45
13	Street Children and the Law in Tanzania	48
14	Street Children and Structural Violence in Latin America	53
15	Street Children in Countries in Crisis: Iraq	55
16	Street Children and Natural Disasters: Sri Lanka	59

Foreword

The *State of the World's Street Children: Violence* examines the pervasive nature of violence within street children's lives and the extent to which their experiences are universal. As the first global report focusing on street children, this is an important piece of work to help us, as activists, practitioners and policy makers, understand the effects of violence on children and how we can better support them.

Preventing and reducing the violence that children are forced to experience will eliminate significant factors pushing them onto the streets and will improve their quality of life. This report shows that to put the blame on poverty is a simplistic approach to a complex problem. If poverty and poverty alone were the cause of children ending up on the streets to fend for themselves, then why is it that millions of children do not abandon their impoverished homes for the streets? Very often the root causes are violence in the home and community; not just poverty. It is important that, as individuals and organisations taking responsibility for the care and wellbeing of children, we learn to listen and respond to their problems and needs. By responding to their needs we can help to create a safe and positive environment that allows children to learn and grow.

No one knows how many street children there are in the world. Estimates have been as high as 100 million. The true numbers may never be known. But do the numbers matter? Isn't one child abandoned to his or her fate on the streets of New York or Cairo or Bucharest one child too many? Some governments continue to believe that violent tactics are an effective method of dealing with street children. Most others pay lip-service to street children, sympathizing with their problems but not investing in resolving those problems. Instead of finding solutions governments are compounding the violence street children face and creating additional hurdles for children to manoeuvre past in their efforts to survive. However, governments are not alone in their negligence and it is an unfortunate tragedy that international agencies ignore these children in their policies and programmes.

As responsible agencies and individuals we must work collectively to listen to the voices of children and to find solutions. Preventing and eliminating violence against children are vital steps for improving children's lives and providing them with a safe, secure environment in which to grow and thrive. As this report shows, we need to do much more to realise a world where children have a voice, where children have a choice and are protected from abuse and neglect.

Alex Dressler
Executive Director
Consortium for Street Children

Executive Summary

This *State of the World's Street Children: Violence* report aims to promote a better understanding of street children's lives and encourage policy-makers, activists, community leaders and service providers to take effective actions to prevent and reduce violence experienced by street children.

The first global report of its kind, *State of the World's Street Children: Violence* also aims to establish a platform for collective research in order to steadily improve the data available for policy-making and developing integral protection systems for street children.

Five key findings underline this report:

1. Street children accumulate numerous experiences of violence from an early age and in a range of environments. Their high risk of exposure to multiple abuses is consistently overlooked in policy development and service delivery for street children.
2. Street children's experiences in countries across the world are strikingly similar, including those in rich countries with child protection systems alongside children in poorer countries which have weaker support structures.
3. Understanding street children's exposure and responses to violence is key to developing integrated preventive and protective policies and services which nurture children's resilience.
4. 25 years after street children first made the international headlines, governments around the world continue to use violent tactics with street children, which contravene their rights, exacerbate their experiences of violence and scapegoat them and their families.
5. Civil society approaches have matured during this period, introducing inclusive methods of supporting children, families and communities to reduce the risks of violence in street children's inter-connected environments.

The report makes **six central recommendations:**

1. **CHILDREN at the centre:** Policy makers, community leaders and service providers must work to secure a social protection system with a wide variety of options for supporting street and other children who have experienced multiple abuses and created a variety of coping strategies. Services should be personalized, offer protection from violence, counselling to address past violence and strategies to protect themselves from future violence. Communities should work with all stakeholders to foment an inclusive approach to child protection in the locality. Read Chapter 2 and Recommendations 1-3 (p. 15)

2. **Support for FAMILIES:** A culture of violence-free households should be a central goal. Public policies need to prepare and support people for parenting and ban all violence in the home. Safe houses are needed for victims of home-based violence and so are services which help families create supportive home environments. Families and street children should be supported to prepare for and achieve reunification. Communities should facilitate reintegration of street children and promote inclusive practices for those children unable or unwilling to return home. Read Chapter 3 and Recommendations 4-10 (p. 22 to 23)

3. **Connected COMMUNITIES:** Investment to develop community-based organizations and linkages between them in poor neighbourhoods is fundamental to reducing local violence. Schools should be inclusive, affordable and violence-free. Community-based organizations should foster neighbourhood social connectedness, working to ensure access to local support services by children and families who do not access them on their own. Read Chapter 4 and Recommendations 11-17 (p. 30 to 31)

4. **STATE protection:** A culture of respect for children must be introduced and sustained in institutional services and public spaces. Police and staff at all levels of the juvenile justice and welfare systems need adequate training. Sanctions should be imposed against individual officials who infringe children's rights. A national Ombudsperson for children should pursue and publicize reports of state violence against children in detention, care and public spaces. Legal aid should similarly be provided to press successfully for resolution of accusations of violence against street children. Street children should be supported to build positive support networks to reduce their exposure to violence in dynamic and unprotected environments. Read Chapter 4 and Recommendations 18-22 (p. 41) on public spaces. Read Chapter 5 and Recommendations 23-29 (p. 47) on institutions

5. **Inclusive SOCIETY:** Poverty and inequality in wider society need to be addressed to reduce violence and prevent children from needing to work or survive on the streets. Integrated schemes involving reallocation of resources from wealthier groups and regions should develop poor neighbourhoods and protect excluded families from external shocks. Community-based organizations and service providers should be instrumental in supporting families and protecting children, including new arrivals, in times of instability in wider society. Read Chapter 5 and Recommendations 30-35 (p. 57)

6. **Strengthened RESEARCH:** An international body should be charged with coordinating and improving the availability of data associated with street children and risks of violence. Country-level data collection and analysis should measure outcomes that matter to street children. Service providers should record information about individual children's exposure to and involvement in violence. Mechanisms for hearing children's voices should be resourced to research and make recommendations about street children and violence. Read Chapter 7 and Recommendations 36-40 (p. 69 to 70)

This report explains how street children accumulate a range of experiences of violence, from an early age. No single recommendation will prevent children from experiencing violence or protect street children who have already experienced violence from further abuse. Effective strategies must address the wider environmental system, of family relationships, community and society within which each child develops and with which he or she interacts. This *State of the World's Street Children: Violence* report concludes in Chapter 6 that preventing children from taking to the streets means preparing children, families, neighbourhoods, services and governments to reduce violence and provide supportive environments for children's development. Protecting street children from further violence means preparing police forces and detention and welfare centres to eliminate violence and nurture children's mental and physical health, working together with families, neighbourhoods and civil society organizations. Prevention and protection require far-sighted policy-making with adequate financial and human resources for community support and effective service delivery.

Introduction

This *State of the World's Street Children: Violence* report is the first in a series of annual reports to be produced by the Consortium for Street Children. The series has two main aims:

- To promote a better understanding of street children's lives and of civil society initiatives to support them.
- To propose effective actions by governments, communities and civil society that prevent children from exposure to risks which cause them to work or live in public spaces and that protect children who are on the streets.

This, the first global report to focus on street children, recognizes violence as a core theme underpinning children's presence on the streets, shaping their experiences in public spaces and influencing their lives. Drawing on leading academic research and up-to-date practical evidence from around the world, *State of the World's Street Children: Violence* is designed to be read and acted upon by policy-makers, activists, community leaders and service providers. Setting the tone of the series, this report is concise and well-referenced, available in print and electronic formats, with links to relevant websites and the Consortium for Street Children's own website (www.streetchildren.org.uk) for additional material.

Street children are globally recognized as children particularly at risk of violence (Pinheiro, 2006: 13) and UNICEF's annual State of the World's Children reports have for many years highlighted the extremely difficult circumstances in which children work and live in the streets of our towns and cities. But despite their visibility, street children have more often served as tragic illustrations of neglect and vulnerability than as genuine targets of policies, programmes and services. Street children are a powerful rallying cause, but enthusiasm wanes with the realization that street children's situations are complex and that quick fixes are rarely a helpful response. Impatient governments and service providers have all too often launched poorly-designed, under-resourced policies and services which fail to help, or even to reach, street children. Labelled a 'social problem', street children have sometimes found themselves at the sharp end of short-sighted policies which appear to protect wider society from 'antisocial' children instead of protecting children from societal violence. Within the world's discourse of respect for children's rights, street children are still treated with brutality by repressive laws, policies and state officials, and are sent regularly to detention centres where abuse and neglect exacerbate the accumulated effects of previous violence.

This report is well-timed. The international community is mobilizing around the issue of violence against children, while civil society initiatives for street children have matured and academic research has advanced, allowing us to start developing a responsible collective voice to support street children worldwide. As the first in the series, this report has weaknesses which will be for future reports to address. In particular: children should participate more directly in report development and greater attention should be given to child-led initiatives; evidence from a wider range of countries including 'rich' countries needs to be addressed; research methods need to become more focused, systematic and rigorous; and criteria for 'good practice' involving street children need to be crafted to provide responsible guidance on putting recommendations into practice.

The definition of 'street children' is contested, but many practitioners and policymakers use UNICEF's concept of boys and girls aged under 18 for whom 'the street' (including unoccupied dwellings and wasteland) has become home and/or their source of livelihood, and who are inadequately protected or supervised (Black, 1993). The concept includes street-living children who live and sleep in public spaces as well as street-working children who work on the streets during the day, returning to their family homes to sleep (Szanton Blanc, 1994; Gomes da Costa, 1997), but leaves out street families, seasonal street workers and others. Definitions continue to evolve to try to capture the fluidity and differences in children's circumstances, including terms such as 'street-connected children' and 'children in street situations' (see Rizzini, 1996; Thomas de Benítez, 1999). This report adopts a recent, more inclusive operational understanding of street children as children for whom the street is a reference point and has a central role in their lives (Rede Rio Criança, 2007: 18).

A similarly broad concept of violence is adopted, in order to accommodate street children's complex experiences of violence, as victims, witnesses and perpetrators. The World Health Organization (WHO) and the International Society for Prevention of Child Abuse and Neglect (ISPCAN) provide a framework (**see Fig. 1**) that recognizes complex patterns of violence. Their typology classifies violence by type – as self-directed, interpersonal or collective – and by the nature of violent acts – as physical (including corporal punishment), sexual, psychological or of neglect.

Fig 1: A Typology of Violence

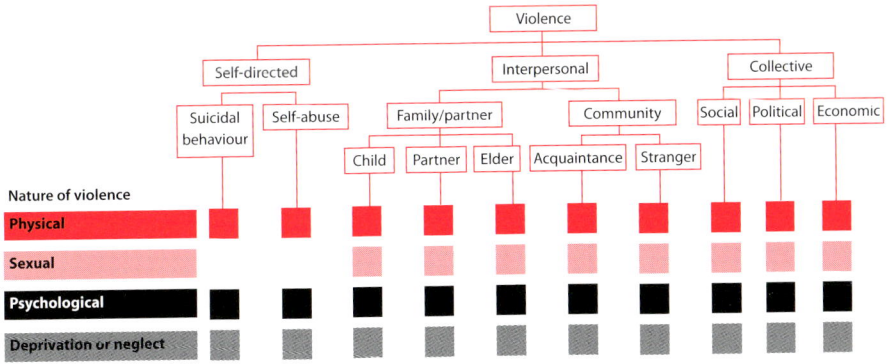

Source: WHO-ISPCAN (2006) Preventing Child Maltreatment: A guide to taking action and generating evidence

This *State of the World's Street Children: Violence* report was developed during the course of 2007 in consultation with the Consortium for Street Children's (CSC) secretariat and members through the CSC Violence Working Group, with support from an expert taskforce. Report content was created in stages: an initial literature review, country papers on street children and Non-Government Organization (NGO) case studies were commissioned; and three draft versions of the report were reviewed by the expert taskforce, CSC member agencies and field partners. An external review of the final draft followed by five academics and practitioners experienced in the fields of violence and street children. Photographs were selected to match the CSC's ethics and ideals: each from a photographer with a distinguished record of commitment to and rights-based work with street children.

69 country papers on street children were commissioned with attention both to: regional representation (29 African countries; 16 from Asia; 14 from the Americas; 6 from Europe and 4 from the Middle East and Oceania); and levels of human development using the Human Development Index (UNDP, 2006). 8 (13%) of 63 countries ranked as 'high' on human development were selected, together with 41 (49%) of 83 countries ranked as 'medium' and 20 of 31 (65%) ranked as 'low' on the Human Development Index. The 16 case studies were commissioned from leading NGOs under the following process: expressions of interest were invited in open tender for case studies covering a range of themes; responses were analyzed and NGOs selected on the basis of agreed criteria by the author and CSC secretariat, supported by the expert task force.

This report starts by introducing in Chapter 1 the 'ecological model' as a device to organize and interpret the evidence gathered about street children's experiences of violence around the world. Each of the subsequent chapters presents: evidence drawn from research and service providers working with children in street situations; case studies submitted by experienced non-governmental organizations working with street children; and recommendations for policies, community support and service delivery. Guidelines to practical applications of each recommendation will be the product of a subsequent CSC research project, and will be available on www.streetchildren.org.uk by the end of 2008.

Chapter 2 focuses on the child, distinguishing the individual from the socially constructed collective label of 'street children' and recognizing that each street child has a unique story of violence. The key role of home-based violence in street children's lives is addressed in Chapter 3, together with the argument that families should be supported to help them eliminate home-based abuse. Chapter 4 explores sources and the nature of violence experienced by street children in 'the community', which in street children's lives comprises at least two communities: the home neighbourhood and the public spaces in which children work and sometimes sleep (often far removed from their original neighbourhood). Chapter 5 explores the vital role played by society in street children's lives, both through services provided for street children in society's name (detention facilities, welfare shelters and other care facilities), and through wider expressions of violence which permeate a society. Chapter 6 draws attention to the commonalities of experiences of accumulated violence by street children/ runaways across countries, and provides evidence of how street children's experiences of abuse increase their risks further. Chapter 7 concludes with a discussion of the methodological difficulties in producing statistics about street children, and presents a first, tentative, Statistical Table: Societies and Street Children, drawing on internationally available cross-country data about children and violence. The aim of the Table to identify country-level indicators of intervention areas which could help reduce the risks of violence to which street children are exposed. A bibliography provides full references to all theoretical and empirical literature cited in the report.

Young boys living off the streets in Phnom Penh, Cambodia.
Photo: Karen Robinson

1

Violence and Street Children
An Ecological Model

1.1 The world of violence and street children is complex. This report shows street children accumulate a range of experiences of violence from an early age. Evidence is strong across countries: children survive abuse at home in fragile families; live in poverty-afflicted, chaotic neighbourhoods; their access to educational and health services is erratic, discriminatory and exclusionary; they confront risks in the street, experiencing violence in their premature entry into the world of work; subjected to abuse and neglect in detention centres and welfare homes designed to protect them, they are stigmatized and shunned by mainstream society. Children who work or live on the streets are recognized as being particularly at risk of violence (Pinheiro, 2006: 13).

1.2 A theoretical model is needed to organize and interpret the practical evidence presented about street children from around the world. Introduced in the late 1970s by Bronfenbronner (1979) and Belsky (1993) for the study of child abuse, the 'ecological model' is still being refined as a conceptual tool. A key strength is that it helps distinguish between the many influences on violence and at the same time provides a framework for understanding how these influences interact. The ecological model recognizes that human beings operate within connected or nested environments: the home (primary relationships), the community and wider society (**see Fig. 2**) in what can be thought of as a 'constant process of reciprocal interaction' (Jack, 2001: 185).

1.3 As well as providing a credible theoretical framework for presenting and interpreting empirical evidence about violence and street children, the ecological model is a useful tool for public policy. Adopted by the World Health Organization for its World Report on Violence and Health (Krug et al., 2002), it subsequently underpinned the World Report on Violence against Children (Pinheiro, 2006: 13). A key implication of the ecological model in terms of policies and service provision for street children is that to be effective, prevention of violence and protection of children who have experienced violence must be holistic. 'No single factor drives violence, either at the level of the

Fig. 2: Ecological Model for Understanding Risk and Protective Factors of Violence

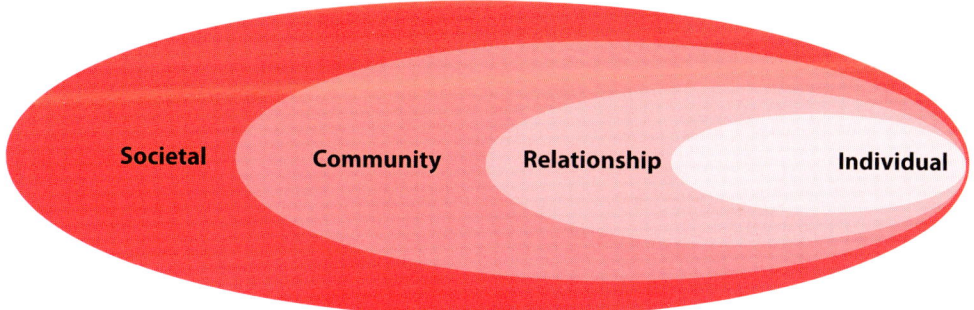

Source: WHO (2002) World Report on Violence and Health. Geneva, World Health Organization

community or the individual. Violence arises out of a complex interplay of individual, relationship, community, societal and political factors' (WMA, 2003). In other words policies and programmes must address the wider environmental system (of family relationships, community and society) within which the child develops and with which he or she interacts.

1.4 In the lives of street children, factors in the family, neighbourhood and public spaces can exacerbate or diminish the risks and consequences of violence (Burgess and Garbarino, 1983; Tan et al., 1991). Within each family, a constellation of factors including the characteristics and personal history of parents and children interact, some enhancing others reducing the potential for violence (Tomison and Wise, 1999). Neighbourhood, street and wider societal stresses such as poverty, inequality, unemployment, lack of public order and security exacerbate such risks. But if the right combination of protective factors can be brought to bear, the outcomes for a child may be positive, even in what seems a generally negative environment (Jack, 2001).

2

Street Children as Individuals
Young Lives and Violence

2.1 Street children have accumulated experience of violence in many areas of their daily lives, sometimes from a very young age. Combined and compounded effects of abuse and deprivation undermine their chances of developing into healthy young people and adults. Each street child has a unique story of violence. This section distinguishes the individual child from the collective of 'street children', exploring agency, resilience and coping strategies.

2.2 'Street children' is increasingly recognized by sociologists and anthropologists to be a socially constructed category that in reality does not form a clearly defined, homogeneous population or phenomenon (Glauser, 1990; Ennew, 2000; Moura, 2002). 'Street children' covers children in such a wide variety of circumstances and characteristics that policy-makers and service providers find it difficult to describe and target them. Upon peeling away the 'street children' label, individual girls and boys of all ages are found living and working in public spaces, visible in the great majority of the world's urban centres. A key factor is their high risks of exposure to violence from multiple sources.

2.3 Gender, age, ethnicity and disability influence the risks of violence to which street children are exposed and their responses to violence. For example, street boys tend more to replicate violence as aggressors and report more physical violence (Raffaelli, 2000), while girls tend to internalize violence and may be more vulnerable to on-going abuse and victimization (Barker et al., 2000). Girls also tend to be vulnerable to additional forms of violence in crisis situations when compared to men and boys (The African Child Policy Forum, 2006) and more likely (although by no means exclusively) to be subjected to sexual violence, often with limited access to preventative measures and other health services (see Van Bueren, 2007). Younger children's relative physical weakness can expose them to violence from older children and adults, although they can also attract protection. Ethnic differences stigmatize some children on the street more than others, making them more vulnerable to violence. These and other variables interact, while each child's risks and responses change over time. In such circumstances, evidence of children's personal experiences is crucial to planning social interventions and to evaluating their effectiveness. NGO work described in this section (see **Case Study 1 and 2**), and throughout the report, demonstrates consistent participation of children and evidence of their experiences in service planning, implementing and evaluation.

2.4 Street children are typically portrayed as excluded by society. While this is not in dispute, such portrayals are in danger of ignoring children's abilities to plan, control their actions and navigate within their environments - in other words their agency. Evidence from countries around the world demonstrates that street-working and street-homeless children regularly plan and put into practice survival strategies, navigating risks and taking opportunities presented within on-street and off-street environments (see for example Burr, 2006; Van Blerk, 2006; Evans, 2006; Stephenson, 2001). Effective strategies to protect street children must address their exclusion and must also recognize street children's agency by ensuring their meaningful participation in design, provision and evaluation of services for which they are the intended beneficiaries. NGO Aparajeyo's practice in Bangladesh, described in **Case Study 1**, aims to reduce child sex work by prioritizing children's participation so that they can influence their own and others' lives.

Case Study 1

Street Children in Bangladesh

The NGO Aparajeyo Bangladesh and its partner ChildHope, have worked together on a 3-year action based research project with nearly 1,000 street children victims of sexual abuse and exploitation in Dhaka City, Bangladesh.

400,000 children are thought to live on Bangladeshi streets[1]: Poverty, abuse and family breakdown are common factors forcing children to leave home and flee to the streets. There, they face harassment, psychological and health problems, including malnutrition, substance abuse, and sexually transmitted infections. Children survive as they can: rag picking, begging, stealing and, worse still, involvement in the sex industry.

Up to 29,000 street children are victims of prostitution[2]; 50% to 75% are girls[3]. Although sexual abuse and exploitation of children are widespread[4], these are taboo subjects in Bangladeshi society and rarely acknowledged. Child sex workers are excluded, branded as outcasts by their communities, abused and exploited by 'pimps', street vendors, gangs and police. Few services are available to these children in Bangladesh[5].

Aparajeyo Bangladesh (AB) and ChildHope (CH) work together to protect and promote the rights of Children who are Victims of Sexual Abuse and Exploitation (CVSAE). As a result of action-based research to identify behaviour change motivators in CVSAE, AB and CH implemented a project with CVSAE in Dhaka City. They hope this pilot will become a replicable model of practice for future work[6]. Activities focus on reducing the incidence of sex work, raising awareness around safer sexual practices, improving living and health conditions, and promoting community tolerance and understanding.

Phase 1 of the pilot, which started in 2002, was to build trusting relationships with children on the streets, carried out by project social workers and peer educators. They visited places popular among street children (parks, markets and transport terminals), developed a rapport over time and informed children about the project. Since then, nearly 1,000 street children (approx 75% girls and 25% boys) have availed themselves of the project's services.

Sheuli fled to the streets of Dhaka after she was raped by her step-father. A man promised her help but sold her to a brothel. She escaped and went back to the streets where she met AB social workers. With their help she trained in embroidery. She was reconciled with her mother and AB visits them regularly to check on Sheuli's welfare

The project's success lies in prioritizing children's participation so they can influence their own and other children's lives. Key achievements of this approach have been that children:
- Became 'Peer educators', promoting safe sex practices and providing advice.
- Got involved in engaging the community.
- Took part in the Joint Management Committee (a children's committee).
- Were actively involved in all the project meetings and workshops.
- Created, supervised and used their own 'Children's Development Bank'.
- Organized public events, covered by the media.
- Started up small enterprises (such a thriving flower shop in the city centre).

Not only were children encouraged to make their own choices, think positively about the future and find alternatives to commercial sexual exploitation, they also gained relevant education and skills development training. As a result:

- 105 children (42% of the total involved) gave up sex work.
- 72 children graduated from the non-formal courses, 10 children were admitted into formal schools.
- 62 girls were successfully placed on internships in garments factories
- In response to 9 children's wishes, the project assisted them in setting up their own self-employment initiatives.
- 10 children established two business ventures with project support.

Sumi escaped from her home when she was 15 because of her violent stepmother. She lived in a Dhaka park, became addicted to drugs and was raped by a policeman. In 2002 she enrolled in the CVSAE programme, receiving medical treatment, counselling and support. Sumi has since become the manager of the Children's Development Bank started under this project. Her dream is to be a social worker.

AB and CH have also challenged community attitudes, raising awareness and promoting acceptance through local meetings, workshops and events. As a result, leading members of the local Dhaka community (professors, doctors, business people and religious leaders) have become a source of strength and support, advocating for reform of government policies and practices on child abuse and sexual exploitation.

The success of the pilot project has allowed work to develop further and new services to be established at children's request, including a 24-hour safe shelter has been opened, offering basic healthcare, counselling, education, child-child support, family tracing, social integration and follow-up services.

Written by: Catherine Klirodotakou, Programmes Officer and Marta Persiani, ChildHope Intern, ChildHope UK (www.childhope.org.uk)

2.5 Psychological research about street children has shifted emphasis from portrayals of vulnerability and dependency to discussions of children's coping strategies and resilience in the face of adversity (Panter-Brick, 2002). There is some debate about whether street children are more or less resilient than other children. Evidence from Colombia suggests street children have low levels of mental illness (Aptekar, 2004) and are resilient to violent experiences. But low self-esteem, depression and self-hatred have also been found to be characteristics of street-homeless children in other settings (Kidd, 2007; Jones et al., 2007; Batmanghelidjh, 2006). That children can learn to cope in dangerous street conditions is not under dispute, and some street children show well-developed abilities to navigate street risks. But coping and resilience is not the same thing: resilience refers to the ability to respond and adapt positively in adverse situations, while coping strategies are behaviours which may be either healthy or harmful to the child's development. A child who copes with violence by running away may be more resilient (if the coping strategy is a healthy and proportionate response) or less resilient (if running away signals inability to cope) than the sibling who stays home. Evidence from NGOs and researchers in the field suggest that street children can display creative coping strategies for growing up in difficult environments (Veale et al., 2000: 137; Beazley, 2003). However, substance abuse is also acknowledged to be a primary coping mechanism among street children (Raffaelli, 1999; Sherman et al., 2005; World Bank, 2007). Resilience enables children to master difficulties and to develop healthily; resilience is also known to vary under changing conditions and to be modifiable by environmental factors (Luthar, 2006) and as such subject to influence by policy and social interventions. There is broad consensus that promoting resilience early in development is more cost-effective than treatment to repair disorders once they have crystallized (Luthar, 2006). It is important to note however that a focus on resilience could be interpreted (incorrectly) as implying individual pathologies and deficiencies in children. A sociological perspective would argue for a focus on mental and physical health, with emphasis on building children's social aspirations and developing their social capital. Participation by all stakeholders, including children, is at the heart of NGO M'Lop Tapang's work to reduce children's involvement in sex tourism in Cambodia, described in **Case Study 2**.

Case Study 2

Street Children in Cambodia

Cambodia's turbulent history has left a legacy of social problems, including large numbers of street children. One source estimated 10,000-20,000 street-working children[7]; another found 1,050 sleeping on the streets plus 670 returning home at night in Phnom Penh[8]. A study of 'vulnerable' children, including street children, in Phnom Penh found 88% had had sexual relations with tourists[9].

M'Lop Tapang (MT) is a local NGO working in partnership with International Childcare Trust to protect street children in Sihanoukville, Cambodia. As Cambodia's only beach resort, Sihanoukville attracts large numbers of economic migrants and tourists. In 2006 the town witnessed a significant growth in the number of bars and other establishments catering to sex tourists, in reaction to Thailand's increased visa restrictions. As sex tourism in Sihanoukville increases, so does involvement of children. In 2006, MT reported on average 4 suspects per week to the police or to Actions Pour les Enfants[10].

My name is Vibol. I am 13 years old. I have been street living on and off as long as I can remember. My mum died and my dad does not really care about me. [...] We have lots of beaches and tourists here. I can make good money from collecting cans and I used to get presents from tourists and scraps of pizza from them. They often gave me money or bought me coca cola.

I used to hang out with Sambath and Kosal, they made me try glue. That was 6 years ago and I am still struggling with this habit. One boy in my gang, Sok, knew a way of making fast money...he encouraged me to go with him and his friends. They met a German tourist, he was about 30, and he paid them $2-5 to sexually abuse them. I would not join in; I just kind of hung out with them. It happened for 5 nights, behind the sand dunes.[...] After a few months, I saw more kids getting paid to do this. I needed the money and wanted to be like my older mates. The first time it happened, the man took me and my 2 mates to his apartment and made us watch sex movies.... then he started to touch us. It was horrible, he is a bad man, but I wanted the money for glue.[...] I told MT Child protection team and that man is in jail now.

Now I stay every day at MT drop in center, but I still sometimes go out on the streets and use glue. I do not really care that much about myself or my family, I just like moving on, but for now, I am learning at the center, we get nice food, lots of football and dancing.

In M'Lop Tapang's experience, successful prevention requires active participation by all stakeholders: from children themselves, their families, their community, the local tourism industry and local authorities. As well as trained outreach and child protection social workers providing day and night services, MT has found the following strategies for prevention to be effective and child centred, based on its experience since 2003:

ChildSafe: MT implements a ChildSafe (CS)[11] network in Sihanoukville, encouraging locals to take a positive approach to child protection. CS staff select members of the community who witness or facilitate child sex abuse e.g., moto, taxi and tuk-tuk drivers, plus hotel, restaurant and guesthouse staff, and provide one-to-one and group training on child protection, the warning signs and how to report them. Successfully certified members are presented with diplomas, ID cards, stickers and shirts that identify them as ChildSafe members. CS policies are pasted on the wall in every guest room and at reception. MT monitors implementation and offers refresher training. As a result, several suspects have been reported to the ChildSafe team and abandoned children have been brought to MT's centre. CS members report that visibility of their CS membership has helped their businesses receiving more respectable and regular customers.

"ChildSafe: *Good Clients = Good Business*"

Youth Networks: MT's child protection team has over 40 members in its youth networks covering 3 beaches. Each network, made up of street working children, has 4 leaders who receive specialist training to become peer educators. MT partners these youth networks, working closely with them on a daily basis. Their rules are to: Keep their eyes open; Recognise and identify potential risks (e.g. inappropriate touching); Protect themselves from danger by sticking to simple rules; Report concerns to MT and their families; Say no to sexual abuse.

Written by: Maggie Eno, Coordinator, M'Lop Tapang (www.mloptapang.org) and Philippa Loates, Programmes Officer, International Childcare Trust (www.ict-uk.org)

The number of street children in Dar es Salaam is increasing every month. Children who have lost their parents through AIDS are often victims of prejudice and neglect at the hands of their guardians and communities. To survive, some orphans leave their village to beg in the city streets.
Photo: Dieter Telemans

2.6 Recommendations: Street Children as Individuals
Policy recommendations
1. Social policies should work to secure a social protection system with a wide variety of options for supporting children who have experienced multiple abuses and created a variety of coping strategies. Such a system must have guaranteed resource levels and must incorporate children's perceptions and experiences into planning and evaluation.

Service delivery recommendations
2. Services for street children should be personalized. Services should offer children protection from violence, counselling to address experiences of violence, and techniques to protect themselves from future violence. Services should nurture resilience and children's well-being, addressing harmful coping strategies such as drug use and promoting healthy coping strategies which enhance children's current and future health. Street children should participate in planning and evaluation of services for which they are intended beneficiaries, and their perceptions, experiences and achievements should form a key part of service assessment.

Community-based recommendations
3. Community networks and organizations should raise local awareness of street children's high risk of exposure to violence from multiple sources. They should work together with service providers, children and other local stakeholders to foment a positive approach to child protection in the locality.

3

Street Children and Relationships
Violence in the Home
(Co-authored by Anita Schrader)

3.1 Family relationships form a vital development pathway for children. Violence in the family affects each child's development differently, but increases the risk of danger for children in other environments too. Evidence that street children have experienced violence in the home – from active abuse to neglect – is overwhelming, across the world. However, it is important to understand that socio-economic, cultural and community circumstances can undermine the potential of families to care for children. This report highlights the key role of family abuse in street children's lives together with the critical need to support families so that they can eliminate home-based abuse.

3.2 In countries as diverse as Bangladesh and the UK, children, service providers and researchers point to family violence as a key factor pushing children onto the streets. Recent research in Bangladesh found: 'moves to the street are closely associated with violence to, and abuse of, children within the household and local community' (Conticini and Hulme, 2006: 2). In the UK, family conflict and problems at home were found to be the most common factors leading to an under 16-year-olds decision to run away and/or live on the streets (Downing-Orr, 1999; Rees and Lee, 2005; Smeaton, 2005).

3.3 Several of the 16 NGO case studies selected for this report illustrate diverse experiences of violence at home from neglect to sexual abuse, most pointedly the 2 children's cases of physical abuse and neglect recounted by Indian NGO Bal Sakha in **Case Study 3**. Writing about runaways in the USA, Tyler (2000) observes: 'biological parents were the majority of perpetrators for physical abuse whereas non-family members most often perpetrated sexual abuse. […] The pattern of exploitation and victimization within the family may have serious and cumulative developmental consequences […] as they enter the street environment' (Tyler, 2000: 1261). In Brazil, street children have invoked neglect as a significant factor in their migration to the street, talking of a lack of daily routines, restrictions and interest from adults (Butler and Rizzini, 2003). Physical abuse by relatives, following parental death linked to the

AIDS pandemic, has been invoked in Uganda (Young, 2004). In Peru, Ordoñez (1996) found that most street living boys were middle children who had become 'scapegoats' - blamed for causing conflict or stress and maltreated when their families were going through a crisis such as loss of a parent or introduction of a step-parent. Ordoñez's work suggests that children leave home for street life because of changes in family structure within the context of poverty and a wider culture accepting of violent child-rearing practices (ibid). Sexual abuse, violence and emotional neglect exist at all levels of society, but children who live in material deprivation and in fragmented communities may feel they have nowhere to turn but to the street.

Case Study 3

Street Children and Family Violence in India

NGO Bal Sakha works with street children in northern India, in partnership with UK-based NGO Railway Children (www.railwaychildren.org.uk). These are Govind's and Geeta's home stories as related by Bal Sakha staff.

Govind is a 14-year-old boy from Bhopal, Madhya Pradesh who came into contact with Bal Sakha in November 2006

Govind's mother died when he was 5 or 6 - she had been a labourer. Govind has one brother, studying Class VIII. His father works in a factory where his monthly income is 3000Rs (about US$70). An uncle lives with them and earns around 3500Rs monthly as a labourer. Since his mother died Govind's grandmother has been in charge of things at home. His father gets drunk and started to beat him regularly. Govind got very lonely when his mother died. He used to study in Class II, but couldn't complete the year as his father didn't provide the study materials necessary to attend school. Because of this he was badly treated by the schoolteacher, and finally stopped going to school. Govind says he left home because of his father's treatment and his grandmother's neglect.

Govind told us:
> *My grandmother never used to give me proper food. Whenever I asked for food she used to bully me. When my father got back from work she used to say false thing about me and then my father would beat me. Although I used to make some of the mistakes she said, they were not so big that he should beat me so badly. My mother loved me very much but she died very early. Why did God call her so early? If she hadn't died nobody would dare to beat me. Nor would my grandmother scold me.'[translated from Hindi].*

Govind became isolated and withdrawn. We met him when he worked on Patna railway station, where he sold water bottles on the platforms. He earned 50-100Rs a day, money which was sometimes snatched by older children on the platform. *'They were very difficult days and night for me. I never got proper food. I used to spend nights crying. I was very scared, sometimes I wanted to go back to my family but when I thought about the harsh behaviour of my father I dropped the idea.'*

He begged on railway platforms in different cities, from Bangalore to Mumbai. On Patna station he visited Bal Sakha's Open Centre and Night Shelter, then came to our Vocational Centre for training in bicycle repair, where he also gets regular counselling. His mental condition is not good as his experiences at home and on platforms have shaken him badly. Govind takes care of his belongings, is very responsible and keeps himself neat and clean, but has lost confidence. It will take time, skill, love and commitment to get it back.

Geeta is an 11-12-year-old from Aurangabad, Bihar brought to Bal Sakha in May 2000. Geeta's mother died when she was little and her father married again. She was assessed as 4 or 5 when she ran away and was found by the police on the streets of Patna; she was very quiet and scared. It was clear to the police that Geeta had been neglected – she was malnourished and had an untreated skin infection. They brought Geeta to Bal Sakha's residential centre – she was too young, then, to talk about her family.

Some time later she told her story:
My [step] mother used to say she and my father quarrelled because of me – she did not want to take me in with her other children. But my father wanted to take me. After big arguments my [step] mother used to beat me - even when it was not any fault of mine. My father never used to defend me or stopped my stepmother. He was afraid of my stepmother.[translated from Hindi].

Geeta remembered not getting enough to eat. She says she ran away one day while her parents were quarrelling.

Geeta couldn't give us much information about her family. Sometimes she regretted leaving and wanted to go home but didn't know the address. She knew she came from Aurangabad, so we contacted the Aurangabad Police. But even with Bal Sakha following Geeta's case closely, we didn't get any positive response.

> When she was little she used to speak so much about her family. But now she never says anything about them. She never speaks about her emotional difficulties, but hates being scolded and cannot tolerate seeing people quarrelling.
>
> Written by: Sanat Kumar Sinha, Chief Coordinator, Bal Sakha, Patna, Bihar, India

3.4 Within psychology, there are several theoretical explanations for the huge damage caused by violence and abuse in the family. One of the most widely accepted accounts is provided by Attachment theory (Bowlby, 1969; Howe et al., 1999). Attachment is a two way bonding process that forms between infants and caregivers. If infants and later children feel secure in the love of at least one carer, they will form a belief (or 'internal working model') of their own worthiness, the generally benign availability of other people, and of themselves in relation to other people. This will help shape their sense of self-worth, behaviour, relationship style, social competence and engagement with the social world (Ainsworth et al., 1978). The obverse is also true. Infants or children who are rejected, who experience a highly unpredictable or even abusive response from their caregiver develop attachment styles that are shaped by these early experiences. An enormous amount of cross-cultural research evidences relationships between children's experiences of maltreatment and rejection, and their subsequent emotional, social, cognitive and even physical development (WHO, 2002). Parents' ability to form secure attachments with their children may be undermined by their own history, and there is compelling evidence that secure and insecure attachments are likely to be replicated inter-generationally (Parr, 2003; Baumrind, 1994; Holmes, 1996; Howe et al., 1999). 'Often as a result of their own neediness and immaturity, maltreating parents are in competition with their children for care and attention' (Baumrind, 1994: 361). The consequences of attachment difficulties can be remedied in later childhood, adolescence or adult life, but the process is more challenging when the foundation has not been made in infancy (Howe et al., 1999). It also depends, to a great extent, on the range and quality of other sources of love and support available to children. Although early research on attachment focused almost exclusively on the mother-child dyad, more recent research shows the way in which poverty, particularly urban poverty characterized by social isolation and absence of peri-natal care, undermine the conditions for the formation of secure attachment (see for example CENDIF, 1999).

3.5 Social learning and cognitive theories help explain how violent parent-child relations are shaped by the wider community and society. Social learning theory argues that virtually all learning occurs on a vicarious basis by observing other people's behaviour and evaluating whether this has desirable outcomes (Bandura, 1975). Under this theory, children are abused because parents have learned (from relationships, community and/or wider society) harsh child-management practices which are believed to be effective or will prepare children for the hardships of adult life. Child maltreatment is likely to be more prevalent where it is socially sanctioned and indeed, encouraged. Cognitive-behavioural approaches also focus on the way in which abusive parents perceive the child's behaviour. Many studies have shown that parents who maltreat often have unrealistically high expectations of their children's developmental capacities (Azar et al., 1984) or attribute their children's behaviour to 'bad intentions' (Ordoñez, 1996).

3.6 Violence, neglect and abuse by primary carers undermines children's development and can reduce their ability to care for themselves in later life (see for example National Research Council, 2003). However, the existence of a stable loving relationship with at least one parent or caregiver, or at least having a parent or an adult caregiver present and calm in the midst of trauma, is known to mitigate the effects of violence in children. A mentor or attachment figure, even in later childhood and beyond, has also been found to make a critical difference to children, including street children, in increasing the chances of forming healthy, stable relationships (Ordoñez, 1996; Aptekar, 2004; Schrader, 2005; Barker et al., 2000). NGO service providers are increasingly focusing attention on helping families create appropriate supportive conditions to enable street children to reintegrate into the household (Thomas de Benítez, 2001; Feeny, 2005). In some conditions, family reintegration is dependent on changing community attitudes, illustrated by **Case Study 4's** description of NGO HANCI's work with girl-mothers on the streets of Sierra Leone.

Case Study 4

Street Children and Reconciliation in Sierra Leone

ChildHope and Help a Needy Child International (HANCI) are working in Sierra Leone on a Peace and Reconciliation post-war project to improve the situation of street children, especially girl-mothers.

Sierra Leone is one of the poorest countries in the world[12] and has the highest death rates for children under 5[13]. After 10 years of civil war two-thirds of Sierra Leone's population of nearly 5 million people was displaced[14]. 60% of these were children[15]. During the war, an estimated 5,000 boys and girls were recruited or kidnapped to become child soldiers. Although statistics are sketchy, it is estimated that at least 5,000 girls were used as workers or sex slaves by the rebels[16], with many becoming pregnant. Unlike other children caught up in the civil war, girl-mothers were not considered "ex-combatants" or refugees by the State and were largely excluded from protection and support[17]. Pregnant girls and young mothers, abandoned by their captors and the State, also faced cultural taboos in which childbirth out of wedlock brings shame upon the family; they were considered a negative influence on other pupils, blamed by community leaders for their association with rebels and rejected by families unwilling or unable to feed returning daughters and their shameful progeny. As a result some girl-mothers left their home communities for the streets to try to survive. Once there they joined the growing numbers of children living in the streets[18].

Since 1994, the NGO Help a Needy Child International (HANCI) had been working with vulnerable children in the northern town of Makeni, a rebel stronghold during the conflict. Through its work HANCI recognised the need to address the particular plight of girl-mothers and confront their ostracisation by society. Together with ChildHope, HANCI developed a project with and for girl-mothers, offering medical services and counselling, vocational skills training and childcare, and ultimately and most importantly helping them to reunite with their families and communities. Since 2004, more than 300 girls have been helped to deal with the traumas they have suffered and to access education and training, and at least 94% of them have been reunited with their families. These achievements were made possible by the project's community based approach and successful advocacy campaign. Alongside support for the young mothers, HANCI and ChildHope have worked to change parents and community attitudes. As a first step the project has employed all local staff who understand the issues facing their community, are trusted and are able to interact successfully. By advocating for forgiveness and reconciliation HANCI has secured the support of local chiefs and religious leaders, who now actively participate in the project, and even see it as their own. Support from leaders, coupled with counselling for families and teachers, have positively influenced attitudes towards returning girl-mothers. In the project's first year, 70 girl-mothers enrolled in local secondary schools and 30 started vocational training courses, with commensurate changes in their employment prospects.

The success of HANCI's advocacy campaign reflects effective networking with other NGOs and relevant organizations, and an innovative use of popular community radio stations. They broadcast talk-show programmes featuring girls, parents and community leaders, which publicize the project and influence community attitudes.

Maria was kidnapped and raped by rebels. She became pregnant in 1999, and her captors vanished after disarmament in 2000. Maria's mother refused to accept her, the community judged her for living with the rebels: she fled to the streets. Maria heard about HANCI on the radio; she contacted staff and expressed a desire to return to school. HANCI persuaded the Principal to enroll her and helped with school fees. Staff then traced Maria's mother who, after intensive counselling, accepted Maria and her child home. Attitudes in the community are also changing and Maria feels welcome.

HANCI's and ChildHope's 3-year community-centred approach has been really successful to date in reconciling girl-mothers with their families, and supporting their access to training and education opportunities[19]. It is now entering a second stage, extending to other regions and increasing its capacity to work with 850 street-living girl mothers, their families and communities.

Written by: Catherine Klirodotakou, Programmes Officer and Marta Persiani, ChildHope Intern
ChildHope UK (www.childhope.org.uk)

3.7 Recommendations: Street Children and Family Violence
Policy recommendations
4. Preventive policies should: promote a culture of violence-free households; prepare and support people for parenting; support them in peri- and post-natal periods to promote secure attachment; and introduce family-child benefits.
5. Protective policies should: guarantee provision of tailored interventions to enable families and street children to prepare for and achieve reunification; introduce long term one-on-one mentoring schemes for street children.

Community-based recommendations
6. Community networks, parent education schemes, safe day-care centres and appropriate childcare should be geared to include all families.
7. Communities should work together with service providers to facilitate positive reintegration of street children, foster positive community attitudes towards such reintegration, encourage local participation in mentoring schemes and promote inclusive practices for street children who are unable or unwilling to return home.

Service delivery recommendations
8. Safe houses should be available for victims of home-based violence (mothers and/or children) with tailored interventions for families to prevent violence reoccurring (including mentoring for perpetrators of violence) and to help mothers and children opt in safely to national and community-based services.
9. Street children's reunification with family should be a well-prepared, individually tailored and sensitively supervised process, responsive to parents' and children's concerns. Services should focus on creating a supportive family environment and on preparing children to form healthy relationships.

10. Tailored interventions for street children and youth unwilling or unable to be reunited with their families should include preparation to form healthy relationships, contact with community services and long-term one-on-one mentoring schemes.

"I used to sell candies in the streets. Sometimes I would steal, but mostly I would beg. For a little while I was with a gang, Mara Salvatrucha. I would sell myself as a prostitute for drugs. I used to sleep in an abandoned warehouse here. Lots of street children go there. But I don't go there anymore because of what happened. Nine months ago I was there sleeping. The police came. It was 6:30 in the morning, and they came into the building where we were. They told all the women to get up and that they were going to search us for drugs. Then they took us to the bathroom and told us to take off all our clothes. At first, I refused. I told them they would not want this to happen to their own kids. But they threatened to rape us all if we didn't do as they said. When they didn't find any drugs they let the other women go. Then one of them laughed in my face. He grabbed me and raped me. Another cop raped my friend Jennifer, who is 15. Then they told us to get dressed, and they left. A little while later they came back, bringing us ham and tortillas to eat. They told us not to tell anyone and threatened us if we did."
"Rosario" Guatemala, 2001. Photo: Donna DeCesare

4

Street Children and Violence in the Community

4.1 In street children's lives, the 'Community' envisaged by the ecological model at **Fig. 2** (p. 7) comprises at least 2 communities: the home neighbourhood, including local schools; and the public spaces in which children work and sometimes sleep (often far removed from their original neighbourhood). This section looks first at sources of violence in the home neighbourhood, exploring poverty and community services, drugs and gangs. Secondly, street violence is addressed, particularly violence by police, among street inhabitants and by the public.

4.2 Street Children and Violence in the Home Neighbourhood

4.2.1 There is overwhelming evidence from across the world that children who work or live in the streets come from poor households in poor, and increasingly urban, neighbourhoods (see eg. Lee et al., 2000; Abdelgalil, 2004; Thomas de Benítez, 2001; Schrader and Veale, 1999; Feeny, 2005). Poor neighbourhoods tend to have weak infrastructure with fewer linkages between community-based organizations (such as schools, health centres, day-care options and grass-roots organizations). Fewer organizations and fewer connections between them have been found to raise the risks for children of abuse (Hashima and Amato, 1994). Street children are commonly excluded from schools as a result of fights, aggressive reactions to teachers, or threats of violence to other children, or withdrawn by families unable to pay school fees, buy uniforms or school materials (UNESCO, 2007). Self-exclusion is also common by children who feel intimidated, unable to keep up or misunderstood. But children who experience violence at home and are excluded from school are cut off from a potentially important source of neighbourhood connection and support. The use of corporal punishment in school humiliates children while reinforcing cultural acceptance of violence as a form of control (Newell, 2000). Teacher training and coaching on resolving conflicts creatively has been shown to reduce development of aggression-related processes in the USA (Aber et al., 1998), with implications for other country settings. **Case Study 5** showcases NGO JUCONI Ecuador's work with teachers to develop violence-free environments for street, and other, children in schools.

Case Study 5

Street Children and Community Schools in Ecuador

JUCONI Ecuador's Inclusive Education programme[20] works to reduce drop-out and eliminate school-based violence in local schools.

In 2004, Ecuadorean children reported that schools were violent places where they could expect to be mistreated[21]. Meanwhile, 20% of school-aged children were excluded from education because families had insufficient resources for schooling and/or did not see schooling as relevant[22].

JUCONI Ecuador, an NGO for street-working children and their families in Guayaquil City, partnered by CSC member International Children's Trust in the UK, held focus groups in 2004 for teachers, parents and street-working children to find their perceptions of school. These confirmed high exclusion rates among street-working children. Teachers saw children's rule-breaking and inability to learn plus lack of parental cooperation as responsible. Parents perceived exclusion, whether forced by school or decided by the family, as caused by schooling costs - uniforms, books and school 'quotas' of US$2 a month. Children's main reasons for dropping out were they felt bullied by teachers who didn't like them and didn't want them in their classrooms[23].

Our work with schools is based on understanding that teachers are unlikely to provide stimulating, caring and violence-free environments for children if they do not have positive experiences in their own education and work experience to draw on. So we start with the teachers…

We have worked with the *Luz del Dia* (Light of Day) school since 2004, providing consultation, practical training and accompaniment in planning and implementing changes teachers want to make. Once teachers have collectively planned their aims for each academic year we provide support and training to help them reach these goals. All our training includes information about how children learn alongside reflections on teachers' own experiences of school. Through this supportive relationship, even abusive teachers began to assimilate a different model of interaction with children and parents. Over time, teachers have seen good treatment as more than just instrumental. Some now regard it as a right they can ensure for children. Teachers' responses to street-working children have changed, exclusions have greatly reduced and academic performance has improved by children with behavioural or learning difficulties.

In 2004, teachers at this school thought street-working children behaved badly and needed firm discipline, including violence. Teachers admitted tying children to their chairs, hitting and humiliating them. Meanwhile, the most common reason given for excluding a child was that parents were not responsive.

Coming to the end of a 3 year process with *Luz del Dia* school there are still many problems, but teachers now set out to resolve them.

> *...we needed to realise what we can do ourselves. There are lots of children who come to this school, then they leave and what have we done for them? We know what happens in their homes and this neighbourhood and we can't change that but we can do something while they are with us in school. We should find ways to use the resources that we ourselves have, that each of us has.* Adriana Alvarez, School Principal

And teachers say they have learned lessons: *'I have made mistakes out of ignorance.'* [...] *'I have had to learn to control my emotions.'* [...] *'I can have a transcendental influence on a child's life.'*

14-year-old Hector and his 5-year-old brother Walter were street working children attending this school in 2004/5. Hector received racial abuse from his teacher and was often told *"you are only good for picking up rubbish"*. Hector's punishment was often a slap to the head and an instruction to pick up school litter. Walter was smacked to 'correct' his behaviour and sent to stand in the corridor if he cried. When their mother complained to the Principal she was told her children lied. Walter refused to go to school after 4 months in First Grade. Hector attended but his grades were poor and he failed the year.

3 years later things are different: Hector has moved up to secondary and Walter is again in primary: *"Now I'm ok here. I have a teacher who helps me. She doesn't call me names"*. His mother agreed: *'Now I'm not afraid to go and see the teacher [...] she is interested in how my child is doing in school and wants him to do well.'*

Other street-working children agree things have improved:
'I feel better than last year although I still don't understand much' Carlos (shoe-shiner, aged 10). *'I understand what the teacher wants now and now he doesn't punish me for bad work'* Maria Angelica (flower seller, aged 8).

Written by: Sylvia Reyes, Executive Director, JUCONI Ecuador (www.juconi.org.ec)

4.2.2 Numerous studies have shown that neighbourhood social capital – the existence of formal and informal social networks – is associated with lower levels of child abuse (Runyan et al., 1998; Garbarino and Kostelny, 1993). Social relationships, particularly with neighbours, community associations, religious networks, close friends and relatives, positively affect family functioning, parent-child interaction and child development (Dunst and Trivette, 1990; Jack, 2001). Conversely, social isolation is associated with an increased risk of child abuse and neglect (Coohey, 1996; Burgess and Garbarino, 1993), and higher levels of physical abuse and neglect of children are associated with neighbourhoods which have lower levels of social interactions. There is still relatively little research on the way in which social networks and social capital in the local community influence children's moves on to the streets (Ferguson, 2005). But we also know that community networks and peers have been found to be important to reducing mental illness in street children (Aptekar, 2004) and street children have been observed to have less balanced social networks and a noticeable lack of helpers compared to other children (Ayuku et al., 2004).

4.2.3 Drug trafficking is reported as a notoriously adverse neighbourhood factor in Latin America, both creating and sustaining violence in many communities and on occasions forcing families and young people from their homes onto the street (Dowdney, 2003, writing about Rio de Janeiro). **Case Study 6** describes drug-related problems in Salvador, Brazil where NGO Viva a Vida's approach to drug rehabilitation fills an important gap in social services for street children. Drug use among family and neighbourhood peers has been consistently associated with drug use by street children in Mexico (Gutierrez and Vega, 2003).

4.2.4 Individual street children sometimes join neighbourhood territorial gangs which can afford them protection and temporary shelter. These groups may be exclusively dedicated to criminal activity such as the quadrilhas in the peripheries of Brazilian cities (Lucchini, 1999), although there is also evidence of street children joining innovative and non-criminalized Arbat system youth communities in Moscow (Stephenson, 2001). The longer term careers of street children within both organized crime and non-criminalized subcultures are under-researched.

Case Study 6

Street Children and Drugs in Salvador, Brazil

Viva a Vida is a NGO Drug Rehabilitation Programme for street boys and boys at risk in Salvador, Brazil.

Brazil changed from a drug trafficking corridor between Colombia-Peru-Bolivia and the USA, to a significant consumer country in the 1980s[24]. Now, the main drugs trafficked and used in Brazil are cocaine, crack, marijuana, amphetamines, LSD and, in smaller quantities, heroin[25]. In Brazil's notorious urban *favelas* or shantytowns, the drug economy has flourished as drug lords and heavily armed gangs bring in money and unprecedented violence. By 1990, in a country of pronounced income inequality[26] and poor job prospects[27], 30% of Brazilian adolescents lived in extreme poverty[28]. *Chacinas* or massacres are increasingly common as well-armed drug traffickers struggle to control *favela* territories. 13 of 16 boys interviewed by NGO Viva a Vida knew at least one person killed directly because of drugs and trafficking in their neighbourhood.

For some youngsters, drug trafficking has become a lucrative option. More are consumers due to unsatisfactory psychosocial conditions. Drug use among street children in Brazil in the 1980s was limited mainly to glue sniffing and marihuana, but more and more children now consume harder drugs. In the north-eastern city of Salvador consumption patterns among street children are changing: Crack - a highly addictive and destructive drug – has become popular. A mixture of cocaine base and baking soda, with the appearance of crystal, crack is known locally as *pedra* or rock. Extended crack use results in depression, anxiety and a decreased appetite for food. It can also lead to brain haemorrhaging, delusions, hallucinations and respiratory problems[29].

> "When I used, I would get into a panic... then when the effect wore off, that thing would hit and you'd want to use more. [..] Each time I used more I would get thinner, I wouldn't eat, I was in bad health, coughing, with a lot of catarrh in my lungs" (Anderson, 13).

Parts of Salvador's historical centre are now known as *cracolândia* - crack-land - where users and dealers congregate. Street children are drawn here, to buy the best crack crystals and beg or thieve from tourists to finance their habit. Realizing that many tourists hesitate to give money, street children ask instead for milk powder to feed their families, exchanging one tin of milk powder for a crack crystal.

The media has targeted street children and youth as responsible for street crime, reflecting widely-held perceptions in society. The 1980s and 1990s saw a rise in numbers of street children and youth killed by police and death squads; the majority of those killed were young, Afro-Brazilian males[30]. Similarly, public policy towards drug-using street children encourages harsh policing and detention in remand centres. Drug-using Afro-Brazilian street children and youth have become scapegoats for a society seeking quick solutions to escalating crime rates associated with drug trafficking.

12 of Viva a Vida's 16 interviewed street boys reported violence at the hands of police: *"They slapped me on the face and stepped on my foot. [...] I felt like a nothing, a shit. I began to think that he only did this because I was black. To a white child he would not do this"* (Pedro – 16, caught smoking marihuana by the police).

By May 2007, 78 drug-dependent boys aged 11 to 17 had used Viva a Vida's services. Most started consuming aged 8 to 12 and most have used several drugs: 96% had habitually used marijuana; 88% crack; 69% inhalants (glue, paint thinner, etc.) and 60% cocaine.

The NGO believes drug rehabilitation must form part of successful intervention strategies for substance-abusing street children, a need largely overlooked by public policy and service providers. Viva a Vida provides therapeutic and educational interventions for substance-abusing street children aimed at helping them understand and address their addiction, gaining educational tools to build productive lives. During 6 to 18 months residency, children work sequentially through Viva a Vida's *10 Strategies for Quitting Drugs*. Using therapeutic activities to stimulate behavioural change, each child is accompanied to work through difficulties and learn new forms of expression. Group and individual therapy, psychiatric treatment, relapse prevention, conflict resolution training, schooling, sports, art and vocational training are all aspects of treatment, as are family therapy and educational seminars in which child and family learn new ways of interacting to improve their chances of successful family reintegration. A 3-year psychosocial after-care programme is in place for child and family to receive support and counselling in facing the challenges of living without drugs.

Written by: Gisella Hanley, Ph.D, Founder and Executive Director, Viva a Vida – Brazil
(www.vivaavida.org)

Street child selling flowers after midnight in Guayaquil, Ecuador. Photo: Marcus Lyon

4.3 Recommendations: Street Children and the Neighbourhood Community
Policy recommendations
11. Social policies should promote investment in developing community-based organizations and linkages between them in poor neighbourhoods, with a particular focus on community-based schools, day-care and other services to support parenting.
12. Schools should be made inclusive and violence-free, introducing effective anti-bullying policies. Schooling costs for families should be abolished, or at least reduced.

Community-based recommendations
13. Community-based organizations should foster neighbourhood social connectedness and encourage development and maintenance of informal support networks.
14. Community-based organizations should adapt drug prevention and other schemes aims at reducing local violence to operate at the neighbourhood level.

Service delivery recommendations
15. Services should provide training for schools on implementing non-violent, inclusive classrooms and on anti-bullying techniques. Services for excluded

children from school should be provided in collaboration with schools and other community-based organizations.
16. Mechanisms should be introduced to ensure access to educational, day-care and family support services by families who do not access them on their own.
17. Drug rehabilitation services should be introduced for children.

4.4 Street Children and Violence in the Street

4.4.1 Violence against children in the street plays out in public places and so receives more attention than the many other environments in which street children experience abuse. Much of the violence experienced by street children in public spaces is attributed to police, and other risks of abuse come from street inhabitants and members of the public. Street children's relations with street gangs and drug use are amongst those areas which are evolving rapidly, influenced by cultural change and drug availability.

4.4.2 There have been many reports across the world of police violence against street children in public places (see for example Human Rights Watch, 2001; Dowdney, 2003; Wernham, 2004; Pinheiro, 2006; UN OCHA, 2007). Periodic round-ups of children, extortion, threats, physical abuse, victimization, rape and murder by police officers have been documented time and again by street children, service providers, the media, lawyers and researchers, as illustrated in the Ugandan case study by NGO 180° Alliance showcased in **Case Study 7**, which links police violence to a street-sweeping campaign in anticipation of the Commonwealth Heads of Government meeting in November 2007. Possibly the most notorious police atrocity against street children was what became known as the Candelaria Massacre in Rio de Janeiro Brazil, when six street children were murdered by gunfire on 25th July 1993, some of them as they slept on the steps of the Candelaria Church. 3 years later, a member of the Military Police was convicted for his part in the massacre. Another rare victory for street children was an Inter-American Court on Human Rights ruling on 13th June 2001 which ordered the State of Guatemala to pay a total of more than half a million dollars to the families of five street children who were brutally tortured and murdered by two National Policemen in June 1990. Known as the 'Bosques de San Nicolás Case #11,383', this was the first case in the 20 year history of the Court where the victims of a resolved case were children. NGO Casa Alianza presented formal accusations of murder in 1990 but it took 11 years of persistent lobbying and campaigning by the NGO and its supporters to secure this historic victory (see www.casa-alianza.org.uk for this and details of other Casa Alianza publications on torture and executions of street children). Police violence against street children remains widespread across the world: 'Street children and youth encounter more violence from the authorities than [do] other children. Street children are beaten, tortured, sexually assaulted and sometimes killed' across the world (UN OCHA, 2007: 30). Such violence may be state-sponsored or attributed to 'rogue elements' in the police force. Guatemalan NGO CONACMI's work with police, described in **Case Study 8**

is designed to improve treatment of street children and to influence wider institutional police culture towards children and adolescents.

Case Study 7

Street Children and State-sponsored Police Violence in Uganda

180° Alliance is a global Christian faith-based action network formed in 2005 to work with street children with the aim of improving service provision, incubating strategic and innovative approaches and influencing policy makers. Toybox is a UK charity founded in 1992 which supports work with street children in Latin America.

Violence against street children in some countries, such as Brazil and Guatemala, has always been in the international spotlight, but governments the world over have rejected, victimised and persecuted street children rather than let them be seen by international leaders and the media. As Uganda prepares to host the Commonwealth Heads of Government meeting in November 2007, Kampala's authorities prepare to remove children from the streets of Uganda's capital city. Their concern has increased as drought, famine and insecurity in the Karamoja region to the North-East of Uganda have forced Karamojong children down to Kampala, swelling the numbers of street children in the capital.

In December 2006, facilitated by UNICEF, the Ugandan Government began consultations with NGOs over their draft strategy for dealing with this problem. The government's draft strategy proposed a scaling up of their approach of forcibly rounding up street children and removing them to Kamparingisa National Rehabilitation Centre (KNRC) - a juvenile detention centre out of the city - before resettling them in Karamoja.

Street children in Kampala already have direct experience of the Kampala City Council's (KCC) techniques: *"KCC usually rounded us up, beat us and took us to Kampiringisa where we would sleep on the floor, and sometimes go hungry. We weren't taken good care of"* (Pulkol). *"While on the streets, I faced a lot of harassment from older people who called me a useless and stupid thief. I was often beaten up by KCC"* (Nassande). *"Sometimes Kampala City Council officials would come and hold us wearing gloves as if we had contagious diseases. They would make a face as if we were too smelly"* (Amei).

Alarmed by the prospect, NGOs in Kampala lobbied the government to change their proposed strategy and called for a halt to the forcible round-ups of street children. Instead they asked for resources to help NGOs provide holistic support to rehabilitate and resettle street children in a sustainable way which respected the children's rights.

Ignoring NGO requests, the Ugandan Government started rounding-up street children and adults again on 4th February 2007. NGOs estimate that on day 1, around 500 children and adults were rounded-up and subsequent round-ups continued throughout the week[31]. Children were taken to KNRC juvenile detention centre, a series of desolate concrete buildings with limited space and very few resources. Street children traumatised by police round-ups found themselves locked in a centre where inadequate conditions further compromised their human rights.

10-year-old Nabale was one of the street girls who ended up in KNRC[32]. Nabale had arrived in Kampala about 3 months earlier, with an Aunt who later abandoned her on the streets: *"I ate leftovers from the market, like potatoes that fell down and nobody noticed"* Nabale recalls. Now in KNRC, Nabele waits to be returned to Karamoja.

NGOs in Uganda continue to advocate for policy changes including an end to police round-ups and use of the KNRC centre for street children. At the same time they continue to lobby for more investment in the Karamoja region and for alternative strategies to help street children in sustainable ways.

Brutal tactics designed to 'clean streets' in advance of international events just prolong and perpetuate problems for children, denying them access to basic human rights. The international spotlight should, instead, be welcomed as an opportunity for governments and civil society to showcase services protecting street children's human rights and helping them gain access to the services and resources they need.

Written by: Andy Sexton, Chairperson, 180° Alliance (www.180degreesalliance.org) and Angela Murray, Advocacy Coordinator, Toybox (www.toybox.org)

Case Study 8

Street Children and Police in Guatemala

CONACMI is Guatemala's National Association against Child Abuse (Comisión Nacional contra el Maltrato Infantil)

In 1996, as Guatemala emerged from a bloody civil war lasting more than 30 years, people thought the Peace Accords would bring an end to violence. One of the objectives of the Peace Accords was reform of the National Police Force (PNC), which had been heavily implicated in repression of civilians. Some reforms have already been achieved, but parts of the PNC are considered to be deeply compromised by, and enmeshed with, violent organized crime[33]. Nonetheless, within the police force, there are different cultures and attitudes to treatment of vulnerable children, as the following incident shows. This is a case reported to the PNC and CONACMI in February 2007; the narrator is a 16-year-old street-living girl:

I was in Bolivar Ave at around 1 pm, when four traffic police came up and frisked me for no reason. After that they beat me. They called the PNC and those frisked me too. They got me to climb into a pickup truck, took away my glue, spilled it on my stomach. That was on Sunday 11th February 2007. Then they shoved my friends into the van, took us to Naranjo Bridge and released us.

Later that afternoon I and six friends were coming from a church that helps us, when we saw one of our companions in a PNC radio car. Suddenly two more police cars appeared. Two police jumped out of the car where our friend was, and told us to climb in – we couldn't do anything. They took us to an alleyway behind the electricity company. We were so scared. As they drove we begged the police not to throw us from the Incenso Bridge. The two other patrols appeared behind us. Suddenly our car swerved into the ring road and headed for the Naranjo Bridge. The policeman driving told us not to be scared. When we got to the bridge, they parked, let us out and said they weren't like the other police, who wanted to 'disappear' us. Before the other patrols appeared, we ran until we reached a bus that took us to Bolivar Ave.

Attacks on street children, including reports of murder and torture by police are part of a wider pattern of human rights violations, rooted in the war[34]. In this climate, the National Association Against Child Abuse *Comisión Nacional contra el Maltrato Infantil* (CONACMI), in partnership with the Consortium for Street Children and supported by the British Foreign and Commonwealth Office, began training the PNC to work with children and young people who depend on the street for survival.

The project was called **'Children's Rights and Child Protection Project'**. We began with action research which actively involved the PNC from the beginning. CONACMI conducted a survey of police attitudes and beliefs about street children and then asked street children in the city centre about their work and lives. Children's perceptions were compared with those of police and with police files. The baseline studies were presented to the PNC and Guatemala's Ministry of Governance.

This action research project helped to secure commitment by the Guatemala City Centre's police force. In the following eighteen months we trained 300 officers in Guatemala City. We also contributed to developing a new curriculum for the police division in charge of children and adolescents, known by its acronym DIANNA. We also assisted the PNC in drafting a child protection policy, which was presented to the Ministry of Governance for approval.

Our project was expanded in 2006 – 2007 to include 635 agents and officers in seven provinces, including five border provinces where people seek to cross illegally into and out of Guatemala on their way to Mexico and, finally, on to the USA. Children separated from adults end up living on the streets there, while others help their families through street work. They are often treated by the police as delinquents, rather than people with rights.

In order to promote institutional change, we also invite senior PNC officers to join our newly restructured National Forum for Street Children. As the incident reported above shows, not all police officers are corrupt or irresponsible and many want to contribute to children's wellbeing. Our work to change the way police deal with street children would have been impossible without the committed support of good people within the PNC. Some officers do good work that is invisible to many. Through them and with supportive training we can gradually influence the wider institutional culture to the benefit of children and adolescents.

Written by: Miguel Angel López, Director, CONACMI - Guatemala's National Association against Child Abuse (conacmi@concyt.go.gt and conacmi@itelgua.com) with Dr. Anita Schrader McMillan, HSRI, Warwick Medical School

4.4.3 Street children are often involved in mutually supportive relationships, with solidarity and self-support amongst children's groups more prominent than violence, an important point made by experienced researchers concerned that over-playing violence between street children can in itself stigmatize and isolate street children (see for example Ennew, 1994; Lucchini, 1996; Bar-On, 1997) and distort policies. However, violence between street children is also commonly reported. Evidence from the Democratic Republic of Congo, for example, highlights abuse of newly arrived street boys and girls who undergo a 'baptism' of hazing by or servitude for older street boys, in which physical and sexual abuse have been reported (HRW, 2006: 34). Gangs of street children and youth have traditionally been fairly transitory and loosely formed (see for example Lucchini, 1997). They may overlap with, but are not the same as, the 'mara" youth gangs in the Americas, drug cartels or de-mobbed child soldiers. Presence of these latter groups can heighten overall levels of violence on the streets and increase risks of 'social cleansing' by armed forces or police. NGOs approach on-street violence among children in different ways, illustrated in **Case Study 9**. NGOs such as Streets Ahead in Harare, Zimbabwe work together with children's informal groups to build supportive on-street social networks.

Case Study 9

Street Children and Violence in African Streets

NGO Street Child Africa (SCA) has worked with a range of long-term partners in Africa for nearly 10 years. In SCA's experience, on-street violence among children is commonplace across countries: for a child to survive on the streets, he or she learns to live within a world of gang hierarchies, systematic bullying and random violence.

Accra, Ghana:
Most younger street children (between 7 and 10) attending SCA partner, Catholic Action for Street Children's drop-in centre say beatings at the hands of older teenage street children are a daily experience. Children report threats and beatings at the hands of older boys on the street; often seen by market women and public bystanders who don't intervene. Such violence enables older children to dominate younger ones and so exert some control over living and working conditions. Age-driven hierarchies are perpetuated as children to the street are socialized into street-based violence.

Port Harcourt, Nigeria:
Children are regularly subjected to violence by gangs '*cults*' of street children who exercise fierce control over work:

I no longer find it easy to work in the market; the bigger boys won't allow us unless we give them N100. Since we cannot afford to pay, there will be no work for the whole day. The stubborn boys amongst us sneak into the market, but get a serious beating if they are caught. At night, we have to sleep in the market park where the big boys search our pockets and collect our day's earnings after which you are permitted to work in the market the next day. If they find no money on you, you get a thorough beating and would not be allowed to work the next day -Gift, a 13-year-old street-living boy in Port Harcourt, who participates in services offered by SCA's partner, Street Child Nigeria - Daughters of Charity.

Street Child Nigeria's centre has received street children cut after beatings with broken bottles in reprisal for breaking unwritten working limits. Every day, two or three street children turn up at the centre with such injuries.

Ndola, Zambia
Drug use is regularly reported as a source of violent flare-ups between street children by SCA partner The Rainbow Project. In Zambia, as in many other countries, street children sniff glue and petrol to stave off hunger and keep warm at night. A distilled mixture of petrol and glue, called *"bostic"* is a high-value commodity for street children. A Rainbow Project street worker tells of a fight between street youth:

Again the fight we witnessed was between two 21-year-olds, Moses and Jones. The boys were uncontrollable as they were fighting over 'bostic'. The latest incident took place on 1st April 2007. When one boy, Victor, intervened in the fight trying to separate them, Jones took the opportunity to run away. Then Moses, upset by the intervention, picked up a very big stick and hit Victor on the upper right eye, provoking a deep cut. Victor had to go to Ndola Central Police to denounce the matter and to get a medical form so he was able to go to the hospital for treatment.

Harare, Zimbabwe
Street children in Harare often live in gangs whose members work together, support each other and sleep in one place, called a *base*. The *base* is fiercely protected from outsiders, including other street children. Each gang has a leader who is feared and respected by the other gang members. He is usually the best fighter - his power earned by his fighting abilities – and may have a violent character. Younger gang members sometimes work for their leaders, who take their money, food and clothing, often without consent. Through the efforts of NGOs like Streets Ahead, SCA's partner in Zimbabwe, these gangs come to tolerate each other. Children from different gangs come to our drop-in centre, spend the day together, mix and form friendships which can even extend to sharing access to their *bases*.

Children have to be strong to survive on African city streets. They are socialized into using and accepting violence as a legitimate way of life. Street gang hierarchies both protect and inflict violence. Intimidation is the order of the day. Younger children are at the mercy of violent behaviour, risking losing earnings and possessions to older, bigger boys. As they grow, they in turn socialize new children into street-based hierarchies and rules enforced by violence. SCA's partners all work with street children to help them manage their anger and reduce violence between children and gangs on the streets.

Contributors: Catholic Action for Street Children, Accra, Ghana
(www.cas-ghana.com)
Street Child Nigeria – The Daughters of Charity, Port Harcourt, Nigeria
The Rainbow Project – Association Pope John XXIII, Ndola, Zambia
Streets Ahead, Harare, Zimbabwe
with Street Child Africa, (www.streetchildafrica.org.uk)

4.4.4 Public hostility and stigmatization on the basis of their appearance and activities are a common form of violence experienced by street children (UN OCHA, 2007: 29). Public hostility is revealed in local words used to label street children them: In Rwanda, 'Mayibobos' in the Kinyarwandan language harbours connotations of 'filth', 'drug use', 'criminality', and 'aggressive behaviour' when used to mean street children (Human Rights Watch, 2003b); in Egypt, a street-living child is a 'sewas', an Arabic word for a small insect that destroys crops (Hussein, 2005: 8); 'throwaways' is a common term in USA for children who have run away from home (Ringwalt et al., 1998); 'Chokora' or 'scavengers' in Kenya (UN OCHA, 2007: 53); and 'Borco' is a collective term found in Ethiopia, which is an adulteration of the Italian words sporco, meaning filthy/dirty or porco, meaning pig (Aptekar and Heinonen, 2003). In **Case Study 10**, Plan Egypt describes effects on the ground for street children of public hostility in Egypt's towns and cities.

Case Study 10

Street Children and Public Stigmatization: Egypt

Around 1 million children are believed to be on the streets of Egypt, most in Cairo and Alexandria[35]. Only recently have the authorities acknowledged the terrible stigmatization to which street children are subjected. A National Strategy for the Protection, Rehabilitation and Reuniting of Street Children was launched in 2003, led by the National Council for Childhood and Motherhood (NCCM) which recognizes that society stigmatizes street children, perceiving them as

criminals rather than children: *"These children are not criminals but victims who have been deprived of their rights – the right to education, health and social care, and especially the right to family care. The strategy is based on changing the way in which society views these children"* **Moushira Khattab, NCCM's Secretary-General**[36].

Society's stigmatization of street children can be bewildering to children who have already suffered violence at home. In Alexandria, Plan Egypt reports: A 15-year-old boy living in Alexandria's Abo Slyman district was hit so often by his father that he left home, found work and started living on the streets:

I am always asking myself about the things that happened to me, did I do something wrong to pay for it every day? All the things that I faced with my father and the persons who I worked with and all the abuse that I faced on a daily basis must be punishment for a thing that I didn't do. [...] I hope to return to school and learn how to change my life and learn how to make people respect me instead of insulting and abusing me.

Although laws describing street children as 'juvenile vagrants'[37] have been replaced, the current 1996 Child Law No. 12 still stigmatizes street children as *'children vulnerable to delinquency'* because a street child fits the following categories 'any person under eighteen who begs, including selling or performing for small amounts of money; collects cigarette butts or rubbish; [...] lacks a stable place of residence; [...] is a habitual truant; [...] lacks a legal source of income or support'[38]. These are 'status offences' which are not criminal acts if committed by an adult. This means street children can be detained not for committing criminal acts but for the failure of others to provide the care and protection they need.

Since 2000 there has been an increase in the numbers of street children arrested for being 'vulnerable to delinquency', with over 11,000 arrests of children in 2001 alone[39]. And there are many examples of ill treatment in police hands: children consider a 'beating' merely as a stage to pass through between detention and release[40].

In December 2006, Egyptian society was shocked out of complacency: a 26-year-old man called Ramadan Abdel-Rahman, known as 'El-Torbini' made headlines after his arrest for raping and murdering more than thirty street children, throwing them off the top of the "Torbini" Cairo-Alexandria express train. This event reminded Egyptian society that street children are unprotected children subjected to appalling abuses.

In Qalubya City, a gang of six street youths called 'Abou Okaz' lived under a bridge in Shoubra El Khema, controlling a group of street children aged 11 to 15 who begged and washed cars for them in public squares. Their bridge was a stone's-throw from the Shoubra El Khema police station. Surprisingly, this gang lived under the same bridge for over 3 years before the police did something about them. Plan Egypt's Qalubya staff see this as symptomatic of how street children's situations are largely ignored by a public and police force who do not see street children as rights-bearers but rather as nuisances.

Even NGO drop-in centres for street children are criticized: NGOs have difficulties finding sites for their centres because communities think these will have a bad effect on the neighbourhood. And there is a view that drop-in centres keep children on the streets, making the problem worse. The argument is that by allowing the child to come and go, letting him back in streets at night, we are making their lives easier and motivating them to stay in the streets. One of the main strategies by the very few NGOs working with street children in Egypt is therefore under attack. And yet, what other options are presented to street children?

A society which stigmatizes street children as illegitimate, immigrant and 'vulnerable to delinquency', allowing them to be neglected by state institutions such as schools and hospitals, and subjected to police brutality, surely should not criticize NGOs for providing shelters for street children.

Written by Plan Eqypt:
Ahmed Shaaban, Community Development Facilitator, Alexandria Program Unit
Sandra Azmy, Street Children Coordinator, Grant Unit
Huessien Hassan, Community Development Facilitator, Cairo East Program Unit
Dr. Reda Haggag, Program Support Manager, Program Support Unit
Dr. Jacinthe Ibrahim, Child Protection & Participation Advisor, Program Support Unit
(www.plan-international.org)
with Andrew Stephens, Volunteer Researcher, Consortium for Street Children

A child who is searching for food at Chowpatti Beach on Easter Day is about to be beaten by a policeman.
Photo: Dario Mitidieri

4.5 Recommendations on Street Children and Violence in Public Spaces: Policy recommendations

18. Policing policies should be reformed to introduce and sustain a culture of respect for children, including training police at all levels and imposing sanctions against individual police officers infringing children's rights.
19. Anti-violence campaigns should be introduced to eliminate public stigmatization of street children.
20. A national Ombudsperson for children should be appointed, fully resourced and with powers to pursue and publicize reports of violence against children in public spaces.

Service Delivery recommendations

21. Legal aid should be provided to initiate, lobby and press for resolution of accusations of violence against street children, including resort to the international courts where necessary.
22. Outreach services should facilitate access to non-violent shelters and to emergency and other support services. Services should work on-street with informal groups of children to build positive support networks to prevent violence and reduce exposure to violence in dynamic and unprotected environments.

5

Street Children and Violence in Society

5.1 Wider society plays a vital role in the lives of street children. Customs and values of mainstream society shape attitudes towards violence, human rights and children. Mainstream society creates conditions which can push families and children to the limit, or an environment in which children can flourish. The State also provides institutions and detention centres which can be highly detrimental to children or can help them towards reintegration. Although shelter care facilities are provided by community level organizations as well as by the State they are located in this section since both State and NGO programmes are provided to act on behalf of wider society. Both are funded through tax contributions and/or civil society donations.

5.2 Street Children and Violence in Residential Facilities

5.2.1 Street children are often removed from the street or encouraged to leave public spaces ostensibly for 'reform', 'rehabilitation' or 'protection'. But their reports of abuse and neglect in detention centres and welfare shelters are received from countries across the world. Accounts of violence against street children in residential centres are commonly recorded in juvenile detention centres and adult prisons (see for example: HRW, 2001; Wernham, 2004; UN OCHA, 2007). Physical, sexual and psychological abuses are perpetrated by guards, adult detainees and other child detainees. Violence in governmental institutions reflects, at best, continuing stigmatization and neglect of street children and, at worst, state encouragement of violence against children. Poor physical conditions and inadequate staffing reflect the low priority awarded by policy-makers to improving street children's future life chances. Abuse in institutions normalizes violence for street children and can exacerbate the effects of previous violence in street children, whether as victims or perpetrators. Bektur's story, told in **Case Study 11** by EveryChild in Kyrgyzstan, illustrates the ease with which unprotected children can be subjected to state detention in conditions of impunity.

Case Study 11

Street Children and Detention in Kyrgyzstan

This is the story of Bektur[41] as told by NGO EveryChild staff members working in Kyrgyzstan. Bektur was a 15-year-old boy found in September 2006 in Karasu City, 25 km from Osh City.

Bektur came to Osh city in June 2006 from Osh province's Alay region to earn money during his school holidays to help his family. There were, he knew, more opportunities to earn money on Osh city streets than in his home town. Bektur's parents were divorced and money was tight at home as his mother looked after Bektur's younger siblings.

Bektur felt lucky when he found a job on a building site owned by an Osh City businessman. Hired as an unskilled labourer, just one of a brigade of labourers without a contract, Bektur was promised 5,000 soms (about US$125) by his boss at the end of a construction job. *"Good support for my family"* thought Bektur.

Three months passed with Bektur living in a nearby abandoned house and working on the construction site. But when the job finished, the businessman said he didn't owe Bektur any money. Bektur was at first stunned, then angry. He grabbed a tape recorder and some other things belonging to the businessman and was heading into Osh city centre hoping to sell the items when he was caught by his ex-boss. Accused of theft, Bektur was taken to the Karsu city detention centre and locked up. His boss had contacts in the police; Bektur knew no-one.

One month later, Bektur was discovered by chance in the detention centre by EveryChild and a team of human rights activists. They were on a visit to the detention centre organized by Osh province's Internal Affairs Department. The visit's purpose was to seek support from international organizations to improve conditions. EveryChild and the team were taken to two cells holding people on remand while they waited for their cases to be processed. Inmates were, they said, allowed out only once a day, to breathe fresh air and use the toilet.

Bektur was found sharing a 2m x 2m cell with five people; Bektur was the youngest, the oldest was 29. The floor was covered by rug on which all six slept. There was an evil smelling bucket in the corner, which served as the makeshift toilet. There were a couple of plastic bottles filled with water to drink and to wash. With no windows the room was lit by a fluorescent lamp. It was September, it was terribly hot.

Bektur took his chance: *"Please help me"* he pleaded with us. *"They do not tell me anything. I do not know why I am here! I am not a thief! He [the businessman] has got contacts here! I do not know who to turn to."*

Bektur's case was immediately referred to Osh province's department of internal affairs for processing. The department head promised to accelerate the process, acknowledging that Bektur had already spent over a month in detention – the legally stipulated maximum time for processing a minor held in detention – and that Bektur's parents had not been informed about their son's imprisonment.

But two months later, nothing had been done. So in November 2006 we referred Bektur's case to the OSCE[42] in Osh.

On 13th of February 2007, on a cold winter's day, Bektur was released from the court room after 6 months in pre-trial detention. He was given a suspended sentence.

Unfortunately, EveryChild was not given advance notice of the trial date. We found out later about Bektur's release. We do not know where he went; he did not even have winter clothes. We contacted social workers in Alay asking them to trace Bektur and his family, but they couldn't find Bektur – we did not have his exact address and had little information about his parents.

We hope Bektur arrived safely home.

Written by Gulnara Asylbekova, M&E Manager
with Ainura Tekenova, Projects Manager, Everychild Kyrgyzstan

5.2.2 NGO shelters and other residential services for street children can perpetuate abuse, if only by concentrating children accustomed to violence in overcrowded, poorly conditioned, under-managed and under-staffed conditions. Researchers have also questioned whether NGOs unwittingly reproduce stereotypes and inferior opportunities for street children (Mikulak, 2003) and it has been argued in the USA that the existence of governmental and NGO shelters for street children may be an incentive to neglect development of other options for street children and youth (Staller, 2004). Child protection policies are in force in many NGOs, they are for example compulsory for membership of the Consortium for Street Children, but on their own they are not enough and systems to protect children from abuse by staff or other residents are sometimes flimsy and unregulated. Violence in detention centres and welfare shelters is an unacceptable reality, in extreme cases denying street children their fundamental right to protection and validating use of violence. Protected children are, however, able to build long-term supportive relationships. NGO JUCONI in Mexico has developed a safe environment to ensure children are protected from violence in its residential care home, showcased in **Case Study 12**.

Case Study 12

Street Children and Protection in Care in Mexico

Junto Con Los Ninos y Las Ninas (JUCONI), which means Together with the Children, is a Mexican NGO partnering UK-based NGOs International Children's Trust, ChildHope and Railway Children.

JUCONI's Safety System protects children and adults from violence within Juconi House, a 'half-way house' residential care programme for boys who have lived on the street.

Our starting point is a commitment to 'Safety First and Always' which requires an understanding by staff and children of:
  a) What constitutes safety and violence (physical, emotional, social and moral).
  b) Why street involved children are prone to violent behaviour.
  c) Treatment needed to foster behaviour that will keep everyone safe.

Children invariably suffer, before living on the street, loss, neglect and/or exposure to family violence as victims, witnesses and/or perpetrators. Street-life further exposes children to traumatic experiences while bolstering defences against emotional pain; defences which cause further violence and deprivation[43]. Together these distort children's abilities to: build relationships; manage emotions; handle change; acquire and sustain positive values. This increases vulnerability to anti-social behaviour and perpetuates violence towards themselves and others[44]. Treatment to heal trauma – causes, not just symptoms – is a powerful tool enabling children to keep safe.

JUCONI's Safety System provides a safe environment, to begin educational-therapeutic work to heal children's emotional wounds.

Our **commitment to safety** establishes expectation of safety as the norm in Juconi House. This means safety issues are raised and discussed freely, risk areas predicted and precautions taken. Risk taking behaviours are explored in workshops and talked about openly and frequently. Supervision takes into account physical areas of risk, like bathrooms and bedrooms, and children's experiences – so some children cannot play with others unsupervised. JUCONI House rules and values, including a strengths-based approach to discipline[45] are displayed and discussed.

Creating a **safe environment** starts with making the physical space clean, organized and attractive. Achieving and constantly maintaining this is a responsibility shared between boys (maximum of twenty-three at any time) and House staff. Since values and habits are acquired experientially, we make hygiene and order our experiential norm. As children and staff together keep their environment safe, a feeling of community develops, helping children internalize JUCONI 'safety' values.

Routines balance high and low-energy activities throughout the day, creating stability using predictability and limits. JUCONI's Safety System includes developing awareness of emotions and capacity to manage and communicate them:

> *At home, my Mum used to throw water on me to wake me up and I used to kick her. I'm learning that isn't a good way to treat someone, but sometimes I can't help doing things the wrong way […] When I am 'on red' my head explodes and I just do things.* -Joel, aged 13, talking to a staff member after he'd lashed out at another child.

Being 'on red' refers to JUCONI House's **'Emotional Thermometer'**, a tool to help children identify their emotional state and control. 'Thermometer' posters are all over the house, running from "I feel fine /calm/ happy/OK and in control" rating 0-3 in the green zone; through amber 's 4-7, indicating stronger emotions and less control; to red's 8 – 10 indicating extreme emotions no longer under control. *"Where are you on the thermometer?"* or *"I am at X on the thermometer because of Y so I need Z from you"*, are heard every day. The thermometer creates a common language for everyone to talk about emotions and how we are managing them.

Children and staff carry pocket-sized, laminated **'safety plans**[46]**'**, containing five actions like "Go and sit quietly on the cushions/Kick a ball outside", aimed to help regain control. Three actions aim to help you soothe yourself; two more actions involve seeking help from someone else. Rodrigo stormed in from work one day, pushed past a staff member, marched upstairs, then stopped and turned back: *"Something happened at work. I'm angry and can't talk. When I've calmed down, I'll look for you."*

JUCONI's twice-daily **Community Meeting** promotes safety and helps manage safety breaches. In the morning meeting, everyone describes how they feel, states their goal for the day and any help they need to achieve it; in the evening they report if and how their 'help' strategy worked. Emergency meetings are convened to address breaches. When Manolo stayed out late, an emergency meeting allowed everyone to say how they felt and how it affected them. Manolo's 'couldn't care less' attitude turned to discomfort as his companions talked about their anxiety and distress; he prepared a written apology to the group for the following meeting.

JUCONI has kept a "Safety Register" since 2004, recording safety breaches systematically to monitor frequency and identify patterns which can help us improve prevention.

Written by: Alison Lane, V.P. Development, Junto Con Los Niños y Las Niñas (JUCONI) Mexico (www.juconi.org.mx)

5.3 Recommendations on Street Children and Violence in Institutions:
Policy recommendations

23. Juvenile justice policies should be reformed to introduce and sustain a non-violent culture of respect for children, including training for staff at all levels and imposing sanctions against individual staff infringing children's rights. Detention must be a last resort, for the most serious crimes and the shortest time possible.
24. The Ombudsperson proposed in recommendation 20 should be fully resourced and with powers to pursue and publicize reports of violence against children in detention centres and welfare shelters.
25. Social policies should give preference to family or community care with professional support over institutional options.

Service delivery recommendations

26. Legal aid should be provided to initiate, lobby and press for resolution of accusations of violence in detention or alternative care against street children, including resort to the international courts where necessary.
27. Alternative care services should develop non-violent, non-custodial, well supervised and child-centred environments to protect children from abuse, envisaged in recommendation 2.

Community-based recommendations

28. Community-based organizations should work together with service providers to support positive reintegration for street children into the community after involvement in detention and alternative care services.
29. Community-based organizations should work with local stakeholders to foment inclusive approach to protecting children who have been detained or in care.

5.4 Street Children and Violence in Wider Society

5.4.1 Writing about street children and endangered youth, Nancy Scheper-Hughes describes structural violence as violence that is permissible and even encouraged by society:

It refers to the invisible social machinery of inequality that reproduces social relations of exclusion and marginalization via ideologies, stigmas, and dangerous discourses (such as "youth violence" itself) attendant to race, class, sex, and other invidious distinctions. […] Structural violence "naturalizes" poverty, sickness, hunger, and premature death, erasing their social and political origins so that they are taken for granted and no one is held accountable except the poor themselves (2004: 13).

This perspective advances the argument that blaming parents for the violence to which they subject their children, or blaming street children for committing violent acts, is making the poor accountable for society's shortcomings. Street children come from some of the poorest and most socially isolated families, often from minority ethnic groups. These families are, under this reading, socially excluded by governmental and/or corporate actions which directly or indirectly exclude some people from participation in mainstream society. Social exclusion is generally understood to involve both process, through which individuals become polarized and socially differentiated, and agency, in which one part of society excludes another (see Burchardt et al., 2002: 6). Poverty does not cause child abuse; the majority of families, even in extreme conditions, strive to care for their children. However, poverty exacerbates stress on already vulnerable families, causing some adults to make instrumental use of children (for example, by forcing them to beg). As noted earlier, poverty and social isolation can undermine the conditions for attachment security. This does not absolve adult caregivers of responsibility: parents who abuse their children are damaging people who are even more vulnerable. Rather, it suggests that blame for abuse and actions to prevent violence cannot be limited to targeting abusive parents, but needs as well to curb wider societal violence. **Case Study 13**, by NGO Mkombozi, describes how in Tanzania, government unwillingness to reform repressive legislation means that children continue to be criminalized simply for living on the streets. children in this way are held responsible for their poverty.

Case Study 13

Street Children and the Law in Tanzania

Since September 2001, Arusha's City Council has ordered periodic police round-ups of street children as 'vagrants', citing a 1944 Townships Ordinance[47]. According to Arusha Council arbitrary arrest, detention and imprisonment of street children is a 'safe and clean cities issue'[48], explained by District Commissioner (2001-06) Fulgence Saria as "legally implementing the regional defence and security committee directive"[49].

Street child round-ups are problematic for at least four reasons: firstly, significant and severe violations of human and child rights occur during the round-ups; secondly, antiquated Tanzanian laws used to justify street child round-ups conflict with tenets of the United Nations Convention on the Rights of the Child (CRC) and with Tanzania's Constitution; thirdly Tanzania's juvenile justice system does not respect street children's rights throughout the arrest, detention, court hearing and remand process[50]; fourthly, local and national Governments consistently fail to provide welfare or development services which would enable children to leave street-life.

Arusha's street children are rounded up on the basis of the 1944 Townships (Removal of Undesirable Persons) Ordinance. This 63-year-old piece of colonial legislation, designed to empower district authorities to exclude "undesirable persons" from their areas, is now being used to arrest street children on charges of 'vagrancy' and 'loitering'. No distinction is made between criminal offences such as theft or assault, and status offences such as living on the street. Street children in need of care and protection are in effect treated as offenders.

At around 1 pm on August 26, 2005, fifteen street children were arrested and taken into police custody. After one night in detention in an adult facility, the children reported being beaten by police officers with a 'caning stick', and were forced to clean the police station and carry large stones on their heads as a means of punishment. Before the children were released back to the streets, they were forced to sweep the court room and cut the court compound lawn (interviews with these children by Mkombozi social workers, September 5, 2005).

Labelling street children as criminal contravenes principles of restorative justice and the best interests of the child enshrined in the CRC. In addition, arrest of a street child under the 1944 Townships Ordinance is arguably unconstitutional. To explain: The offence of 'loitering' is based on the supposed danger a person poses or the assessed risk of an action against community safety, so the loitering offence is premised on suspicions about actions that have not yet taken place. According to legal principle[51], however, without action a person cannot be responsible - and without responsibility, a person cannot be considered guilty. Loitering as an offence is incompatible with a maxim of legal principle and as such is arguably unconstitutional.

Tanzania's ratification of the CRC[52], the ACRWC[53] and the ICCPR[54] means discretionary powers afforded to District Authorities to maintain peace and order must be exercised in harmony with these international principles. However, street

children in Arusha have consistently reported the following characteristics of police round-ups to Mkombozi:
- Arrest of children as young as 12 without warrant.
- Denial of release under bail for detained street children.
- Use of corporal punishment.
- Detention of children in adult facilities.

According to Mkombozi social workers, round-ups of street children in Arusha follow a similar - troubling - pattern: street children are arrested for 'loitering' or 'vagrancy' without warrant; they are detained in police lock-up alongside adult criminals[55]; they are subjected to violence and abuse at the hands of police officials; they are handled without understanding or appropriate services in adult courts; and finally, children are released back to the streets without any productive alternative or link to community services[56].

The lack of legal protection for street children represents a serious violation of humanitarian points of law, including principles of restorative justice, non-discrimination, proportionality, dignity of the person, equality[57], effectiveness, legality and rule of law.

Tanzania's unwillingness to reform dated and repressive legislation with respect to children means children continue to be criminalized simply for living on the streets. They are 'cleaned' from the streets as a public security measure which fails to respect children's rights and fails to address a challenging social problem. Arusha's police round-ups of street children, condoned under unconstitutional and repressive Tanzanian legislation should be condemned for:
- Masking the failure of Tanzanian Government and society to address the needs of street children.
- Reinforcing stereotypes of street children as 'criminals' and 'delinquents' who need punishment and correction.
- Flagrant violations of human rights and the rights of children.

Written by: Kate McAlpine, Director, Mkombozi Centre for Street Children (www.mkombozi.org)

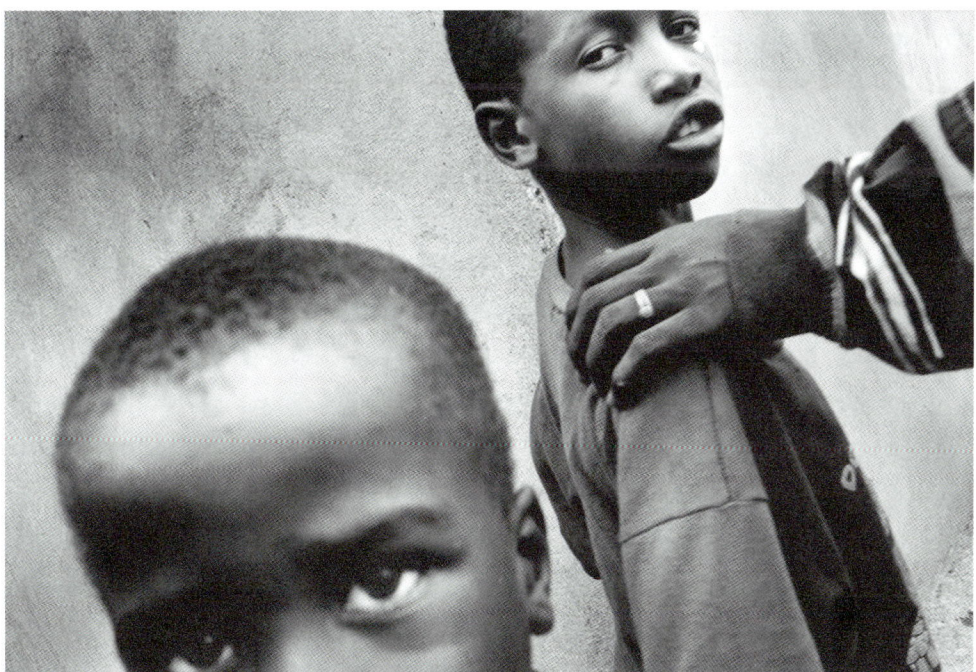
Young boys photographed on the streets of Freetown, Sierra Leone. Photo: Pep Bonnet

5.4.2 When violence is understood as social, implications for social policies and service provision are profound. Family violence, considered in many cultures as a private matter, can be recognized as a clear matter for public intervention. Societies which view children as the property of their parents are ill-equipped to protect children from abuse, while those that emphasize children's rights are likely to experience much lower levels of child abuse (Belsky, 1993; Jack, 2001). Similarly, societies where physical punishment of children is rare or prohibited tend to have significantly lower rates of child abuse (Jack, 2001; Newell, 2000). Only rarely however have governments acknowledged society's multi-faceted role in support for families: 'The primary task of society is to support the family financially, practically, organisationally and psychologically. The main responsibility must lie with both parents, but on the clear assumption that society will in different ways be instrumental in ensuring that this responsibility is exercised in a sound manner' (Norwegian Government, 1995:26 p. 6).

5.4.3 Research in Europe and the USA has consistently shown links between concentrated poverty, high unemployment levels and child abuse (see for example Baumrind, 1994; Graham et al., 1998; Black et al., 1999; Krug et al., 2002). Poverty can be understood in several ways, as for example having insufficient resources to meet household needs for food and access to services such as health and education, or as suffering material deprivation relative to the majority of society. An approach to poverty coherent with the ecological approach to child abuse focuses on capability deprivation (Sen, 1992), which emphasizes not how people actually live or function, but their having the capability (the practical choice) to function if they so wish. An individual or community can be deprived of capabilities in various ways, including but not limited to insufficient income, for example by lack of transport facilities, experience of violence or inadequate legal protection. Conversely, the well-being of an individual or a community can be assessed on the basis of the opportunities they have or choices they can exercise. Street children accumulate experiences of violence in income poor households in income poor, often violent, neighbourhoods, with limited access to basic services, severely constraining their opportunities and choices. In such circumstances the street can offer the tempting illusion of freedom.

5.4.4 Another important factor influencing rates of child maltreatment is the degree of inequality that exists within a society; the degree of economic inequality rather than overall level of prosperity being the crucial factor (Jack, 2001: 187). The position of an individual or family in relation to other members of that society have also been found to make a significant difference to levels of child abuse and outcomes for human development (Wilkinson, 1996). It is not certain that a country's level of income inequality is directly associated with the numbers and conditions of children living in the streets, although empirical evidence from Latin America and more recently Africa suggests that street children numbers are large where economic inequalities are high. World Vision in Latin America puts the case in **Case Study 14** that income inequality causes children to work in street markets to help sustain their families, putting their own well-being at risk. Research in rich countries suggests children's general well-being is negatively affected by income inequality: the USA and UK were ranked bottom and second from bottom respectively of 21 OECD countries in a multi-dimensional measure of child well-being, despite overall high prosperity levels in both countries (UNICEF, 2007). Inequality, rather than poverty, has also been charged with fomenting violence among young people. Research on young men and violence in Brazil has found that:

> Frustration and anger over unequal distribution of opportunities are the breeding grounds for violence, rather than abject poverty per se […]. Where the rule of law does not exist or is fragile, where opportunities for employment are blocked and when individuals experience frustration on a large scale, interpersonal violence - mostly carried out by young men – increases (Barker, 2005: 64).

Case Study 14

Street Children and Structural Violence in Latin America

Children in Latin America account for 35% of the total population, but more than half of these children live in poverty. As a region, Latin America has the highest levels of income inequality in the world; even consistently strong economic growth has not reached many of the region's poorest. Inequalities of wealth have entrenched poverty and homelessness, holding back children's well-being across the region. World Vision believes poverty and wealth inequality are not only acts of violence in themselves, but also generate and encourage violent acts. There are significant gaps in legal and institutional mechanisms to report and denounce structural violence, as well as a lack of interventions to prevent acts of violence[58]. Children who work in public places are exposed to the violence of their neighbourhoods and of their workplaces, even when workplaces such as markets seem to parents to afford some shelter and protection to their children.

Child Workers in the Wholesale Food Markets: Lima, Peru

It is common to see children as young as 4 walking up and down the streets, in the middle of the traffic, selling objects or cleaning windshields. And children as young as 7 carry heavy loads from the early morning hours in Lima's wholesale markets. Most originally came from the countryside; their parents came to the city hoping for a job and a better life. But many end up exposing their children to the misery and violence of work in Peru's capital city, Lima.

Children's routines in the markets include carrying vegetable bags, in carts or on their shoulders, from the market stands to a customer's bus or car outside the market. They arrive at 4 am, looking for early work and carry on till the evening.

From the moment they leave their homes for the market, children are exposed to the street dangers common to the inner-city environments at such hours. They work to support themselves and help their parents. Some work so they can pay their schooling costs (uniforms, materials, enrolments etc), but it is difficult to attend school regularly and work as well.

Some clients say to us, "You're just a child. You shouldn't work". But others do not care about that. Once I had an accident. I was busy loading a cart, and another porter passed by me with a heavy load and hit me. I got a cut and the scar is still there (Marco).

Once, I was hauling a load and when I was going downhill, I was hit by one of the bars in the cart, taking a chunk of flesh out one of my feet. I healed myself at home with herbs. Another time, I almost lost an eye when I banged it. I asked a policeman to help me. He stopped a minibus, and asked the driver to take me to the hospital. At the emergency room, a female doctor came and requested help for me. They told me my retina was damaged. She put a bandage on my eye and told me to come back. But I didn't go back because I had no money (Edwin).

World Vision's Work
Violence is a structural problem that is generating crisis in our societies. The inequity and poverty situation faced by Latin-American families force parents to have their children go work in the streets and contribute to the family income. Children at work have become daily portraits of our cities and neighbourhoods; making it so normal that we are no longer shocked and fail to see the risks and dangers of exploitation that these children have to live day by day.

Preventing violent situations and finding alternative ways for contributing to families' income and sustainability are part of World Vision's approach to help children stay in healthy and safe environments. Using workshops and training sessions for parents and teachers we aim to eliminate child-raising models that promote violence at home and in the community, showing parents ways in which they can better relate to and support their children. We also form part of child protection community networks with local organizations, schools and public institutions that prevent child abuse. Communities themselves can promote surveillance and response systems to crimes, serious aggressions, exploitation, abandonment or negligence, all aimed at reducing violence in the neighbourhood.

The church is one of the fundamental pillars of our work in the communities. We have united with other Christian organizations, developing a theological biblical framework on the topic of children and publishing materials focused on children, theology and our mission.

Written by: Maria Jose Meza; Child Rights Officer and
Maria del Mar Murillo; Regional Communications Officer
World Vision International, Latin American & Caribbean Regional Office (www.visionmundial.org)

5.4.5 When social institutions are stressed and community cohesion breaks down, in times of war, natural disasters, health epidemics or rapid urbanization for example, children's risk of violence grows as protective barriers crumble. In general, violence experienced by society at large is reflected in incidence of violence in the home and in public spaces. More children may be forced on to the streets either to work or live as a result of reduced protection or increased incidence of violence in the family or a combination of both. On the streets they may be faced by higher levels of violence while the capacity of residential facilities to protect children reduces as services become overwhelmed by larger numbers of children. War Child describes the situation for street children in Iraq in **Case Study 15**, adding to the evidence that societal instability increases risks of violence and at the same time reduces protection for children.

Case Study 15

Street Children in Countries in Crisis: Iraq

The security situation in Iraq continues to deteriorate rapidly as a result of increased sectarian violence. Violence which has been mainly limited to Baghdad and other areas in the north is spreading and southern cities such as Nassiriyah that have until recently been relatively calm are now witnessing a spike in targeted attacks by militants. International relief agencies are (understandably) reluctant to operate in such unstable environments, leaving vulnerable children, including those living and working on the streets, with frighteningly little support[59]. In September 2006 War Child conducted an in-depth qualitative study in the southern Iraqi cities of Basra and Nassiriyah with 69 children: street workers, children in detention, girls accused of morality crimes and young drug users (some respondents belonging to more than one category). Our aim was to explore issues faced by these children and to develop recommendations with them. The study's final report[60] concluded that essential needs of the most marginalised children such as street children are not being met – either by Iraq's state system or by NGOs.

Street children who participated in the study usually said they were forced onto the streets in search of work because of poverty and family breakdown (the former often precipitating the latter). Street working children reported they had been unable to continue their education[61] and most children War Child spoke to were illiterate. With employment opportunities scarce, street working children have little option but to accept dangerous and demeaning jobs such as selling drugs or alcohol, pushing carts or searching through rubbish dumps for materials to sell. As 12-year-old Ashraf said: *"We are born to work. This is our life."* Our research team was told of a boy electrocuted while attempting to remove wire from an electric pole to sell and whose body remained on the pole for 3 days. Street working children also talked of exploitation by employers who delayed payments (sometimes for months) while verbally and physically abusing their charges. Some children told us they themselves use violence and aggression as a way of dealing with their circumstances. Street working children also reported sexual abuse at the hands of adults and peers and felt stigmatised by the wider community: during our research one street child drew a picture of a dog, explaining: *"This is how society looks at me"*.

We spoke to Mustapha, aged 10, who reported that he had been so severely abused by his stepfather (his father was killed as a result of sectarian violence) that he felt he had no option but to leave home. Mustapha lived on the streets making a living selling drugs and alcohol. He soon started taking drugs himself, was arrested by the police and sent to a juvenile detention centre, where we interviewed him. Mustapha blames himself for his situation and self-harms regularly to deal with the pain and trauma he suffers. Mustapha dreams of leaving prison and setting up his own shop.

Some children in detention in south Iraq are street working children from dislocated and acutely poor families who come into conflict with the law by working on the streets selling drugs or pornography or engaging in sex work. These children reported being subjected to violence by prison guards and other inmates. Most said that lack of access to schooling had contributed to their imprisonment, along with abusive relationships with family members. 14-year-old Zahir said, *"Prison won't solve our problems. Why don't they arrest our families who have neglected us and abused us instead, or our relatives who have involved us in criminal activities?"* Zahir and others reported that terrorism was making things worse: increasing poverty and creating a climate of violence that affected their own lives.

In 2006, with UNHCR co-funding, War Child awarded grants to twenty local child protection organizations for a number of projects including awareness-raising on issues of violence and discrimination in schools and trained social workers to help them to better respond to needs and advocate for the rights of excluded children. War Child also piloted a livelihoods programme for vulnerable families to protect children by strengthening families' economic capacities. Our 2007 objectives in Iraq are: to continue building local capacity to protect marginalised children including street working children; and to help families in Nassiriyah develop viable livelihoods to prevent children from being forced onto the streets in search of employment.

Written by: Amy Price, Security Coordinator, War Child (www.warchild.org.uk)

5.4.5 Migration and displacement also play important roles in the lives of street children and their families. While presenting opportunities, migration to cities to escape rural poverty can rupture families' kinship ties as well as neighbourhood support networks, while exposure to the increased economic inequalities of city living place a range of new stresses on nuclear families and subject children to new risks, including cultural and linguistic shocks, for which families may be completely unprepared. Displacement, whether triggered by natural or human-led events, may cause dramatic ruptures to family and community life. Vulnerability to violence and the risk of children working on the streets or leaving home for the streets can be greatly exacerbated in such circumstances.

5.5 Recommendations on Street Children and Violence in Society:
Policy recommendations
30. Family and neighbourhood poverty should be addressed through integrated investment, employment, welfare and training schemes including, as appropriate, micro-credit, child benefit and social development programmes.
31. Economic and social inequalities should be addressed through reallocation of resources from wealthy regions and groups in society to enable development of poor neighbourhoods and protection of poor families.
32. Policies should promote support for families and protection for children from external shocks and instability, guaranteeing financial and organizational resources to prevent children being sent to work on the streets or leaving home for the streets.

Community-based recommendations
33. Community-based organizations should raise local awareness about links between poverty, inequality, instability and violence against children.
34. Community-based organizations should receive training and resources in local management of external shocks and instability, to support families and protect children including new arrivals to the area in times of increasing potential for violence.

Service delivery recommendations
35. Services should work with policy-makers and community-based organizations to develop protection for street children from violence and prepare them for reintegration. Services should be prepared to give additional support to children and families in times of increasing instability and external shocks.

6

Conclusion
Street Children and Violence

6.1 Children who come to spend most or all of their lives on the street experience individual journeys of violence. Many of those who do not report experiencing violence within the home have survived other traumas, perhaps as internally displaced migrants, refugees, soldiers or trafficked children. Some have suffered famine, natural disasters, orphanhood caused perhaps by AIDS, social violence or war. But evidence across the world suggests that any of these factors is, on its own, insufficient to cause the contextual ruptures which trigger children's moves to the streets (see for example Ennew, 1994; Bray, 2003). Ill-treatment by extended families, local neighbourhoods or welfare services towards young survivors of home abuse or of natural or man-made disasters may tip the balance. Children orphaned by AIDS in the Democratic Republic of Congo have reported having their inheritances taken by relatives, being accused of sorcery and subsequently abused by religious authorities, before ending up on the streets as a result of these combined experiences (HRW, 2006). On the other side of the world, children in Guatemala have reported intra-family physical and psychological abuse as the trigger for moving on to the streets, where intra-family violence is set within a context of high poverty, high income inequality, low human development, high migration levels and the aftermath of 36 years of vicious civil war which left an estimated 200,000 orphans (Lloyd, 2006).

6.2 Some journeys on to the street and off the street are extremely violent, including those involving child trafficking and participation in war. There have been reports of children being recruited from the street for trafficking or to join armed militia, and also of children moving from those situations on to the street. In Togo for example, street children are one of the four groups considered most vulnerable to being trafficked (HRW, 2003). There are also reports of Togolese girls trafficked for use in domestic or sexual work and boys forcibly recruited for agricultural labour who have escaped or been released from enslavement, and then move on to the streets to survive (ibid). Recent initiatives to help street children avoid being trafficked include training to equip children with the skills to recognize potential risks and resist being trafficked (Plan, 2005). In Myanmar, street children were reported to be the main targets of frequent military round-ups, from which they were taken to holding camps for new recruits and trained for army service (HRW, 2002), swelling the ranks of children in the army. As some street children became child soldiers, so other child soldiers escaped from brutal army life and, as deserters, have taken to street life to subsist (ibid). These children experience appalling violence as victims, witnesses and perpetrators of violence as a precursor or addition to their experiences of street violence. On the other hand, as Sri Lankan NGO Shilpa Children's Trust explains in **Case Study 16**, street children can receive unexpected support from international attention drawn by dramatic events such as refugee crises, de-mobilization of child soldiers or natural disasters.

Case Study 16

Street Children and Natural Disasters: Sri Lanka

Since 1987, Shilpa Children's Trust (Shilpa) has run a rehabilitation centre in Colombo for 50 girls displaced by internal conflict between the Sinhalese majority and Tamil minority. In December 2004 a tsunami devastated the southern and eastern coasts of Sri Lanka, leaving over 38,000 people dead and 860,000 internally displaced[62]. Shilpa was asked by the Sri Lankan government to run a community-based program to help children in the tsunami-affected district of Hambantota.

This is Saraswathi's story, a 13-year-old girl from Hambantota. Saraswathi lived on the streets with her family from the day she was born. Her earliest memories are of hunger and fear. She was frightened by the vehicles whizzing by, worrying constantly about accidents. As she grew older she learnt to beg on her own. Some days she earned Rs. 100 and felt proud of being able to help. She would run to give the money to her mother who would use it to buy rice, sugar, tea and cooking oil. Saraswathi started school but dropped out in Grade 2. From then on she spent her whole day on the streets, although as she grew older she grew more self-conscious about begging.

On December 26th 2004 her father was working as a casual gardener in a nearby hotel. When the tsunami swept over Hambantota, it destroyed the hotel, taking Saraswathi's father away with it. His body was never found. Her mother too was swept away but managed to save herself. Saraswathi was with her five siblings in an unaffected part of town further inland. The next weeks were a daze. Saraswathi's mother managed to find her children as people searched for relatives among the 5,000 bodies piled-up in and around town. The horror and despair of those days brings tears to her eyes.

Two months after the tsunami Saraswathi's life changed dramatically. Social workers from Shilpa, carrying out a survey of children who had lost parents in the tsunami, found the family living in an abandoned hut. Saraswathi's 6-year-old brother Murugesh, whose legs were wasted at birth, lay huddled on the dirt floor, alone and neglected while his mother and siblings begged on the streets.

Shilpa social workers registered Saraswathi and her siblings in the National Child Protection Authority (NCPA) database and opened a bank account in each child's name. By March 2005 each child was receiving a monthly stipend of Rs. 2,500 added to a lump sum of Rs. 500 in a personal savings book. The family of six was housed in a brand new apartment built by World Vision in Hambantota in the tsunami aftermath. A small two-roomed apartment, it has a bathroom, a tiny kitchen and living room – conditions beyond Saraswathi's dreams.

Shilpa helped Saraswathi enrol in a school nearby. Currently in Grade 4, she is 3 years behind her peers but by taking non-formal education classes run by the Education Department she is making up for lost time. At first she was shunned, as the only street child in her school. Shilpa social workers have encouraged Saraswathi to take pride in her appearance, although she has found it an uphill struggle to keep clean, brush her teeth and comb her hair regularly. Shilpa staff also talk regularly to her teachers to make sure Saraswathi feels included. She now has a few friends and is no longer treated as an outcast:

At first I wanted to run away to the streets, but then I also felt ashamed to beg. Now I enjoy playing and talking to the other children. The teachers treat me kindly. [...] Yes, I want to keep on going to school and maybe one day I can be a teacher.

Saraswathi's family life has changed completely: as a street family they did not attract support, but the tsunami focused attention on children like Saraswathi. Thanks to the children's stipends, her mother can stay home and look after her disabled son, Murugesh, who received a wheelchair through Shilpa 2 years ago and is now mobile and cheerful. Murugesh does not go to school. Life is not without problems: Saraswathi's family is still shunned by the other apartment residents, and the children are still harassed in the local playground. Shilpa social workers mediate, counselling the family to look after their apartment and encouraging a more inclusive attitude by the community.

> Shilpa currently supports over 300 children who lost one or both parents to the tsunami. Shilpa also runs children's clubs, dance and art therapy programs, counselling and medical camps in Hambantota.
>
> *Written by: Chandini Tilakaratna, Secretary, Shilpa Children's Trust (www.shilpa.com) with Philippa Loates, Asia Programmes Officer, International Childcare Trust (www.ict-uk.org)*

6.3 Much can be made of differences in the types and intensity of violence experienced by street children between countries and regions; and clearly, policies, community support mechanisms and service delivery must be highly sensitive to children's local circumstances. But the value of this report lies not in identifying particular regional or thematic differences but rather in drawing attention to the commonalities experienced by children who work or live on the streets, as evidenced in: recent academic research; the 16 NGO case studies written in 2007 by leading service providers for street children around the world; 69 country reports commissioned in 2006 as input for this report; and Consortium for Street Children's access to experiences of its 53 NGO members and hundreds of their field partners across the world. More striking than any surface differences are the profound commonalities of experiences of accumulated violence by street children/runaways across countries, irrespective of the overall prosperity of nations: in all parts of the world, most street children have experienced intra-family violence, and come from fragile families located in income poor neighbourhoods.

6.4 Children who have experienced some of these horrors are entitled – morally and legally – to expect support from wider society. But when living on the streets, children experience violence of public places, from public stigmatization (**Case Study 10**), through being shunned by basic services and abused by adults who commercially or sexually exploit them (**Case Study 1 & 2**), to appalling abuse by police (**Case Study 7 & 13**). Contact with criminal justice systems and even welfare shelters can add fresh experiences with violence from staff and inmates, in spaces ostensibly designed to protect them (**Case Study 11**). Across the world, policies and their respective budgets for street children are grossly inadequate, seriously underestimating children's accumulated experiences of violence and the support they and their families need to develop resilience, healthy coping strategies and capabilities to participate in mainstream society.

6.5 Long term effects of accumulated violence on street children are under-researched and evidence to date is mixed. That violence impacts on children's development and life choices is beyond reasonable doubt – a point which has been made robustly to policy-makers (Krug et al., 2002; Pinheiro, 2006). At the extreme, death rates among street children in some countries are reportedly high from homicides, accidents and overdoses (see eg. Hecht, 1998; Casa Alianza at www.casa-alianza.org.uk). Suicide is also reported as often contemplated by street youth (see eg. Jones et al., 2007; Tari et al., 2005), and there is evidence of street children self-harming in various countries (see eg. Sherman et al., 2005; Herrera et al., 2008). Perceptions of multi-sourced stigma by homeless youth in USA and Canada have been related to low self-esteem, loneliness, suicidal ideation, and feeling trapped, and further compromise the mental health of young people already grappling with myriad risks and challenges (Kidd, 2007: 297). There is also evidence that the longer a child spends living on the streets the more remote his or her prospects of successful insertion into mainstream society through a lasting placement in an orphanage or residential home (eg. Huang et al., 2004). And in countries such as Kenya, India and Brazil, families consisting of three generations of street children have been reported (see eg. Droz, 2006). In the absence of alternative models, parenting is likely to draw on their own experiences as children, suggesting the perpetuation of abuse through the life cycle and across generations (Tomison, 1996). But systematic documentation of street children's lives is rare and existing reports tend to look back from the street through early childhood (see eg. Rizzini and Butler, 2003), rather than tracking forward through youth and adulthood, so street children's own parenting as perpetuating abuse is under researched. There is however, a growing understanding among NGO service providers, manifested explicitly in most **Case Studies**, that social interventions which are successful in helping street children overcome accumulated experiences of violence to integrate into mainstream society are child centred, personalized, protective, participatory, involve long-term mentoring, families, schools and communities.

6.6 As recognized and advocated by all the NGO writers of **Case Studies 1 to 16**, preventing children from taking to the streets means preparing children, families, neighbourhoods and governments to reduce violence and provide supportive environments for developing children's capabilities. Protecting street children from further violence means preparing police forces, detention and welfare centres to eliminate violence and nurture children's mental and physical health, their resilience and coping strategies, and working together with families and neighbourhoods. Prevention and protection require far-sighted policy-making with adequate resources for community support and effective service delivery.

A drunken Muscovite takes exception to a street boy begging
Photo: Robin Hammond

Street Children and Violence
Statistics and Methodology

7.1 Street Children and Statistics: An Introduction

7.1.1 Estimating numbers of 'street children' is fraught with difficulties. In 1989, UNICEF estimated 100 million children were growing up on urban streets around the world. 14 years later UNICEF reported: 'The latest estimates put the numbers of these children as high as 100 million' (UNICEF, 2002: 37). And even more recently: 'The exact number of street children is impossible to quantify, but the figure almost certainly runs into tens of millions across the world. It is likely that the numbers are increasing' (UNICEF, 2005: 40-41). The 100 million figure is still commonly cited, but has no basis in fact (see Ennew and Milne, 1989; Hecht, 1998; Green, 1998). Similarly, it is debatable whether numbers of street children are growing globally or whether it is the awareness of street children within societies which has grown. While there are understandable pressures for policies to be informed by aggregate numbers, estimates of street child populations, even at city levels, are often hotly disputed and can distract rather than inform policy makers.

7.1.2 Key methodological problems are discussed briefly in Section 7.2 below. A Statistical Table: Societies and Street Children is then presented in Section 7.3, providing international data about country conditions which, this report argues, are instrumental in reducing risks of violence faced by children. These statistics provide only small and limited windows onto the world of street children and violence. Our aim is to stimulate a systematic search for more comprehensive and focused data to guide policy makers and advocates in eliminating the causes of children leaving home for the streets and reducing the violence sustained by children already connected to the streets. Section 7.4 provides recommendations for research to improve the statistical data available.

7.2 Methodological Difficulties in Producing Statistics about Street Children

7.2.1 Children's appearance in public statistics and social accounting is on the increase internationally. But street children, for all their visibility on urban street corners, have proved elusive to statisticians. There are two main obstacles to counting street children:

definitional difficulties and children's fluid circumstances. These are exacerbated by the broad range of characteristics and activities associated with street children as the main body of this report illustrates. Reliability of data is also highly problematic. Each of these difficulties is described in the following paragraphs.

7.2.2 There is no international agreement on the definition of 'street children'. And the label of 'street children' is increasingly recognized by sociologists and anthropologists to be a socially constructed category that in reality does not form a clearly defined, homogeneous population or phenomenon. UNICEF developed the earliest definitions, which are still in common use by policy-makers and service-providers, identifying two categories of street children: children 'of' the street (street-living children), who sleep in public spaces, without their families; and children 'on' the street (street-working children), who work on the streets during the day and return to their family home to sleep (Szanton Blanc, 1994; Gomes da Costa, 1997). UNICEF's definition was extended in the 1990s to include at least one more category of street children: 'street-family children' who live with their family on the streets (see eg. Droz, 2006 on Kenya and Brazil). But research and practice have surfaced an enormous variation in children's experiences and considerable overlap between these three groups: for example some children live on the streets all the time, others only occasionally or seasonally, while others move between home, street and welfare shelters (see Lucchini, 1996). Some retain strong links with their families; others have broken or lost all contact. 'Runaways' in rich countries such as the UK and USA include children sometimes described as 'detached' (see Smeaton, 2005) who in poorer countries would be considered 'street children'. Definitions continue to evolve, with terms such as 'street-connected children' and 'children in street situations' being used by academics and practitioners (see eg. Rizzini, 1996; Thomas de Benítez, 1999). Recent research in Rio de Janeiro by a coalition of NGOs distinguishes between street workers, beggars, 'inhabitants', 'refugees' and 'tourists', defining street children as children for whom the street is a reference point and has a central role in their lives (Rede Rio Criança, 2007: 18). The wide variety of children's circumstances and characteristics, however, continues to present huge definitional challenges.

7.2.3 Children's use of public spaces is also fluid and may be undetected. Sleeping, working and recreational places may be highly insecure and children may keep out of sight to protect themselves. Girls can become almost invisible (Railway Children, 2006). Children are on the move at work or change base camps, whether to avoid police or other street inhabitants or to improve earnings – leading to both double-counting and under-counting. Working hours during the week, month and year are variable, changing with agricultural seasons, school holidays, public demand, police tactics, friendships, family situations along with other personal and societal factors. Distinguishing children from young adults by observation or even in interview can be problematic. Counting (visible) street children in any given day or night, week or month, can yield dramatic variations in numbers. The lack of fixed locations for sleeping, working and hanging out also presents difficulties for assessing trends in numbers over time: street children counted in one location in one month/year may be quite different in another month/year, as particular children move around and as locations become more or less attractive collectively to children in the streets.

7.2.4 Definitional problems, children's elusiveness and other difficulties in distinguishing 'street children' from other inhabitants of public spaces are compounded by the non-standardized use of data collection methods. Some studies for example count children only found in public spaces, others include street children resident in welfare shelters. These undermine data reliability. Even for basic headcounts, researchers need to be trained observers with a good knowledge of a city's streets, and teams need to be well-coordinated to avoid repeat counting (Aptekar and Heinonen, 2003), since numbers counted in a single city can double, triple or show even greater disparities between studies (see eg. Hecht, 1998). Qualitative research which seeks to understand street children's experiences and circumstances depends heavily on the children themselves as central informants. But street children have a host of good reasons for providing misleading, false or no information for self-protection, even when innovative, non-threatening, participatory research methods are used. Cross-checking (triangulating) interview information with other sources produces more reliable data but is also problematic: street informants can be transitory; families may be far away, unknown to the researcher, or guarded in supplying data about their children; service providers may have children registered under different names and are also heavily reliant on children's own accounts. Meanwhile, fluid lifestyles make observation and maintaining contact with individual respondents over time complex undertakings.

7.2.5 Careful planning, experienced researchers, local informants and adequate resources (including time) are required to collect valid and reliable data. Aptekar and Heinonen's research on street children in Nairobi, Kenya (2003) and government studies in Mexico City (COESNICA, 1992; COESNICA, 1996; DIF-UNICEF, 2000) suggest that careful and transparent data collection methods can transform large 'guesstimates' into more carefully counted numbers of 'street children' with different characteristics and circumstances. Data collection methods, analysis and reports should be widely consulted and coordinated with informal as well as formal service providers for street children. More recent research has also mapped service delivery for street children (eg. Rede Rio Criança, 2007 in Rio and Dynamo, 2005 in Brussels), putting emphasis on number and characteristics of support centres rather than numbers of children.

7.3. Societies, Street Children and Violence: Moving Towards Statistical Analysis

7.3.1 The methodological difficulties inherent in counting street children and the paucity of data produced by quantitative research on the streets encourage a search for data which can better help guide policy-making about street children. This report takes a first, tentative, step at international level by identifying indicators which shed some light on child well-being and protection of children from violence by country. Indicators have been grouped into: indicators of violence directly concerning children; those which relate to violence in the home; and others which are suggestive of levels of violence in wider society. Our choice of indicators reflects both availability of country level data and this report's ecological approach, suggesting that the conditions faced by street children are better understood in terms of exposure to risks of violence than through headcounts. The Statistical Table: Societies and Street Children below presents a selection of country indicators drawn from international publications together with a single column 'Street Children Visibility Level 2006' using information generated about street children from the country papers commissioned for this report. The selection of indicators is premised on understanding violence - at home, in the community and within wider society - as creating and exacerbating the conditions which cause children to work and live on the streets.

7.3.2 The Statistical Table below uses UNICEF's State of the World's Children (SWOC) 2007 alphabetical ranking of countries (Column 1). Column 2 provides a first, tentative, ranking by country of the level of visibility (high, medium or low) of street children drawn from information generated in 2006 about street children from the 69 country papers commissioned for this report. This indicator seeks to replace the estimates of street children populations with the 'visibility' of street children in a country to NGOs, governments, academics and the media. This change in focus is informed by the concept that 'street children' are a socially constructed category, which suggests that estimated numbers of street children may reflect increased awareness of numbers children working and living on the streets rather more than increased numbers of children in street situations.

7.3.3 'Visibility' of street children, by reflecting the level of societal awareness of children living and working in the street, seeks to capture the level of societal interest in street children, while making no assessment of the nature of that interest, whether manifested as repressive, welfare-based or rights-focused. High 'visibility' indicates that children have been detected on the streets in sufficient numbers and long enough to attract sustained NGO, governmental, media and research attention (= known NGO presence + government programmes for street children + media reports + academic research). Low 'visibility' indicates that children have not been detected in sufficient numbers and long enough to attract sustained NGO, governmental, media and research attention. A high visibility classification should suggest to advocates and policy-makers that: children are visible working and living on the streets of the country's main towns and cities during much of the year; data can be found from NGO, government, media and academia to inform advocacy/policy strategies; advocacy and policy-making should be urgently directed at protecting children from violence and reducing existing levels of violence for long-term prevention. A low visibility classification should suggest to advocates and policy-makers that: few children are visible working and living on the streets; data on street children may be available from NGOs, government and academia but may be scarce; advocacy and policy-making may be effectively directed to preventing violence towards children. This first rating of countries using the 69 country papers is speculative. Data were gleaned from available literature, are narrative-based and depend heavily on the quality of the commissioned country papers. To be useful for future reports: the indicator needs to be assessed for its helpfulness to advocates and policy-makers internationally; criteria need to be ordered and clarified; and data collection needs to be standardized. At this stage however, the indicator simply challenges the idea of using 'guesstimates' of 'street children', putting forward an option which captures to some extent societal awareness of children on the streets and therefore of the potential focus for policy-making and advocacy.

7.3.4 Columns 3 to 5 direct attention to general levels of protection afforded to young children, through mortality rates for the under-5s, UNICEF's key indicator of child well-being, extracted from the State of the World's Children (SWOC) Report 2007 Table 1 (p.112 columns 1, 2 & 3; see www.unicef.org). Rankings in Column 1 compare levels of child protection by country while Columns 2 and 3 together suggest progress in protecting children in-country and over time.

7.3.5 Columns 6 to 8 address risks of violence in the family by highlighting 3 indicators: Column 6 reports existence of Official Child Abuse and Neglect Counts (also known as Child Abuse Registers), extracted from ISPCAN's (2006) World Perspectives on Child Abuse (see www.ispcan.org). The maintenance of a child abuse registry was found to correlate significantly with lower child mortality rates (ISPCAN, 2006: 4). Column 7, drawn from SWOC 2007 Table 8 (UNICEF, 2006: 130) assesses the lifetime risk of maternal death (annual number of deaths of women from pregnancy-related causes per 100,000 live births) on the assumption that if mothers' well-being is high, children will have a lower exposure to risks of violence, and vice-versa. Column 8, which reports on whether or not corporal punishment of children is prohibited in the home, is taken from the Global summary of legal status of corporal punishment of children prepared by the Global Initiative to End All Corporal Punishment of Children, updated September 2007 (see www.endcorporalpunishment.org). This indicator offers a crude assessment of whether children are protected by law from home use of corporal punishment, understood as an expression of physical abuse in this report, by the World Report on

Violence Against Children and by the Committee for the UN Convention of the Rights of the Child, is permissible in the home.

7.3.6 Columns 9 to 17 offer indicators suggestive of risk levels of violence for children in their communities and wider society. Columns 9 to 12 address prohibition of corporal punishment of children in schools, in the penal system as sentence and as disciplinary measure, and in alternative care settings respectively. These indicators offers crude assessments of whether children are protected by law from physical abuse in different public environments and are, as Column 8, taken from the Global summary of legal status of corporal punishment of children (www.endcorporalpunishment.org). Columns 13 and 14 explore existence of social policies aimed at reducing violence in society by addressing the existence of a national report on violence and a national policy document on violence respectively. These indicators were taken from the World Health Organization (WHO, 2007: 8). Column 15 lists the 'The Failed States Index' rankings published annually by the Fund for Peace (see www.fundforpeace.org), a composite index intended to assess a country's vulnerability to violent internal conflict and societal deterioration, and as such associated with higher risks of violence for children. Columns 16 and 17 show country rankings in the Human Poverty Index (HPI-1) and the Gini Index respectively, the first a ranking of country-level poverty, the second a measure of income inequality within country, drawn from UNDP's Human Development Report for 2006 (UNDP, Tables 3 and 15 respectively).

7.3.7 This first tentative 'Statistical Table: Societies and Street Children' is provided as a platform for analysis and refinement by better selection plus weighting of key measures in successive future reports in this series. There are, as yet, few internationally comparable country indicators addressing risks of violence to children; data are not consistently gathered, measures are not standardized or are limited to the rich countries (see WHO, 2002; Pinheiro, 2006; World Bank, 2002). Standardized datasets on types, nature and levels of violence in the home and in society across countries could provide a basis for development of benchmarks for reducing risks of violence experienced by children.

7.4 Recommendations for Research
Policy recommendations
36. Create an international body charged with researching, developing and producing international statistical tables capable of capturing country-level variables associated with changes in children's exposure to violence and levels of street children's exposure to violence.
37. Introduce and scale-up country-level data collection aimed at measuring outcomes that matter to street children, including rates of children's violence-

related deaths and injuries, indicators of domestic violence, indicators of violence in schools, in detention and in care.
38. Invite street children specialists, children and street children to participate in research to measure effects of poverty, income inequality, social exclusion, migration and protective barriers on street children and to consider how mechanisms for hearing children's voices should be established and adequately resourced to research and make recommendations about street children and violence.
39. Commission, to inform policies and service delivery: quantitative survey-based research on street children using standardized definitions and methods, and making methods and databases available for research; qualitative ethnographic research with street children about their perceptions, behaviours and experiences of service provision.

Service delivery recommendations
40. Introduce service-based information systems to record of information about individual children's exposure to and involvement in violence to facilitate appropriate coherent case management and tracking of individual street children in services over time. Select indicators on exposure and reactions to violence that can be easily and uniformly recorded for all children who enter the service system.

7.5 A Statistical Table: Societies, Street Children and Violence

		Child				Family							Community and Society				
1	2	3	4	5	6	7	8	9	10	11	12	13	14	15	16	17
Countries and Territories	Street Children Visibility Level 2006[7]	Under-5 mortality rank 2007[1]	Under-5 mortality rate 1990[1]	Under-5 mortality rate 2005[1]	Official Child Abuse and Neglect Counts (Child Abuse Register)[2]	Maternal mortality ratio, 2000 Lifetime risk of maternal death, 1 in:[1]	Corporal punishment of children prohibited in the home[3]	Corporal punishment of children prohibited in schools[3]	Corporal punishment of children prohibited in the penal system as sentence[3]	Corporal punishment of children prohibited in the penal system as disciplinary measure[3]	Corporal punishment of children prohibited in alternative care settings[3]	Countries with a national report on violence [and health][4]	Countries with a national policy document on violence[4]	Failed States Index Rank 2007[5]	Human poverty index (HPI-1) Rank[6]	Gini Index[6]
Afghanistan	-	3	260	257	-	6	NO	NO	YES	NO	NO	-	-	8	-	-
Albania	-	121	45	18	No	610	NO	YES	YES	YES	NO	-	-	111	-	-
Algeria	-	78	69	39	-	190	NO	YES	YES	[NO]	NO	-	-	89	46	35.3
Andorra	-	190	-	3	-	-	NO	YES	YES	YES	NO	-	-	-	-	-
Angola	High	2	260	260	-	7	NO	YES	[YES]	NO	NO	-	-	53	79	-
Antigua and Barbuda	-	140	-	12	-	-	NO	NO	NO	NO	NO	-	-	121	-	-
Argentina	-	121	29	18	No	410	NO	YES	YES	NO	NO	-	-	150	3	52.8
Armenia	-	92	54	29	Yes	1200	NO	YES	YES	YES	NO	-	-	112	-	33.8
Australia	Low	161	10	6	Yes	5800	NO	SOME	YES	SOME	SOME	-	-	169	-	35.2
Austria	-	168	10	5	-	16000	YES	YES	YES	YES	YES	-	-	166	-	29.1
Azerbaijan	-	50	105	89	-	520	NO	NO	NO	YES	NO	-	-	62	-	19.0
Bahamas	-	129	29	15	-	580	NO	YES	YES	NO	NO	-	-	129	-	-
Bahrain	-	146	19	11	Yes	1200	NO	YES	YES	???	???	-	-	134	-	-
Bangladesh	-	57	149	73	Yes	59	NO	NO	NO	NO	NO	-	-	16	85	31.8

Countries and Territories	Street Children Visibility Level 2006[7]	Child			Family			Community and Society								
		Under-5 mortality rank 2007[1]	Under-5 mortality rate 1990[1]	Under-5 mortality rate 2005[1]	Official Child Abuse and Neglect Counts (Child Abuse Register)[2]	Maternal mortality ratio, 2000 Lifetime risk of maternal death, 1 in:[1]	Corporal punishment of children prohibited in the home[3]	Corporal punishment of children prohibited in schools[3]	Corporal punishment of children prohibited in the penal system as sentence[3]	Corporal punishment of children prohibited in the penal system as disciplinary measure[3]	Corporal punishment of children prohibited in alternative care settings[3]	Countries with a national report on violence [and health][4]	Countries with a national policy document on violence[4]	Failed States Index Rank 2007[5]	Human poverty index (HPI-1) Rank[6]	Gini Index[6]
Barbados	-	140	17	12	-	590	NO	NO	NO	NO	SOME	-	-	130	5	-
Belarus	-	140	19	12	No	1800	NO	YES	YES	YES	SOME	-	-	51	-	29.7
Belgium	-	168	10	5	-	5600	NO	YES	YES	YES	SOME	-	-	167	-	33.0
Belize	-	125	42	17	-	190	NO	NO	YES	SOME	SOME	Yes	-	114	-	-
Benin	Medium	21	185	150	Yes	17	NO	NO	YES	[YES]	NO	-	-	104	90	36.5
Bhutan	-	53	166	75	-	37	NO	NO	???	NO	NO	-	-	47	71	-
Bolivia	Medium	64	125	65	-	47	NO	NO	SOME	NO	NO	-	Yes	59	28	60.1
Bosnia and Herzegovina	-	129	22	15	No	1900	NO	YES	YES	YES	NO	-	-	54	-	26.2
Botswana	Medium	37	58	120	-	200	NO	NO	NO	NO	NO	Yes	Yes	119	93	63.0
Brazil	High	86	60	33	Yes	140	NO	NO	YES	NO	NO	Yes	Yes	117	22	58.0
Brunei Darussalam	-	151	11	9	-	830	NO	NO	YES	NO	NO	-	-	109	-	-
Bulgaria	-	129	18	15	Yes	2400	YES	YES	YES	YES	YES	-	-	128	-	29.2
Burkina Faso	-	16	210	191	-	12	NO	YES	YES	YES	SOME	-	-	33	101	39.5
Burundi	High	17	190	190	-	12	NO	NO	YES	NO	NO	-	-	19	78	42.4
Cambodia	High	25	115	143	-	36	NO	SOME	YES	YES	NO	-	-	48	73	40.4
Cameroon	High	23	139	149	Yes	23	NO	YES	YES	YES	NO	-	-	35	61	44.6

Canada	-	161	8	6	Yes	8700	NO	YES	YES	YES	SOME	-	-	168	-	32.6
Cape Verde	-	85	60	35	-	160	NO	NO	YES	YES	[YES]	-	-	66	43	-
Central African Republic	-	15	168	193	-	15	NO	NO	???	???	???	-	-	10	91	61.3
Chad	High	8	201	208	-	11	NO	NO	YES	NO	NO	-	-	5	100	-
Chile	-	150	21	10	Yes	1100	NO	NO	YES	NO	NO	-	-	159	2	57.1
China	Medium	96	49	27	Yes*	830	NO	YES	YES	YES	???	-	-	62	26	44.7
Colombia	High	108	35	21	Yes	240	NO	NO	SOME	NO	NO	-	-	33	10	58.6
Comoros	-	59	120	71	-	33	NO	NO	[YES]	NO	NO	-	-	79	56	-
Congo, Rep of	-	43	110	108	-	26	NO	[YES]	YES	NO	NO	-	-	26	51	-
Congo, Dem. Republic of the	High	9	205	205	Yes	13	NO	YES	YES	SOME	NO	-	-	7	80	-
Cook Islands	-	113	32	20	-	-	NO	NO	YES	NO	NO	-	-	-	-	-
Costa Rica	-	140	18	12	-	690	NO	NO	YES	YES	NO	Yes	-	140	4	49.9
Côte d'Ivoire	-	13	157	195	No	25	NO	???	YES	YES	NO	-	-	6	82	44.6
Croatia	-	156	12	7	-	6100	YES	YES	YES	YES	YES	-	-	127	-	29.0
Cuba	Low	156	13	7	-	1600	NO	NO	YES	NO	NO	-	-	77	6	-
Cyprus	-	168	12	5	-	890	YES	YES	YES	YES	YES	-	-	113	-	-
Czech Republic	-	182	13	4	-	7700	NO	NO	YES	YES	NO	-	-	149	-	25.4
Denmark	-	168	9	5	No	9800	YES	YES	YES	YES	YES	-	-	170	-	24.7
Djibouti	-	30	175	133	-	19	NO	[YES]	???	NO	???	-	-	71	52	-
Dominica	-	129	17	15	-	-	NO	NO	NO	NO	NO	-	-	-	-	-
Dominican Republic	-	89	65	31	-	200	NO	NO	YES	YES	???	-	-	69	27	51.7
Ecuador	High	102	57	25	-	210	NO	YES	YES	NO	SOME	-	-	73	18	43.7

Countries and Territories	Street Children Visibility Level 2006	Under-5 mortality rank 2007	Under-5 mortality rate 1990	Under-5 mortality rate 2005	Official Child Abuse and Neglect Counts (Child Abuse Register)?	Maternal mortality ratio, 2000	Lifetime risk of maternal death, 1 in?	Corporal punishment of children prohibited in the home	Corporal punishment of children prohibited in schools	Corporal punishment of children prohibited in the penal system as sentence	Corporal punishment of children prohibited in the penal system as disciplinary measure	Corporal punishment of children prohibited in alternative care settings	Countries with a national report on violence [and health]	Countries with a national policy document on violence	Failed States Index Rank 2007	Human poverty index (HPI-1) Rank	Gini Index
Egypt	High	86	104	33	Yes	310	NO	YES	YES	YES	NO	-	-	36	44	34.4
El Salvador	Medium	96	60	27	-	180	NO	YES	YES	YES	???	-	-	92	32	52.4
Equatorial Guinea	-	9	170	205	-	16	NO	NO	???	???	NO	-	-	41	69	-
Eritrea	Medium	52	147	78	-	24	NO	NO	NO	???	NO	-	-	50	70	-
Estonia	-	156	16	7	No	1100	NO	YES	YES	YES	NO	-	-	140	-	35.8
Ethiopia	High	19	204	164	No	14	NO	YES	YES	YES	SOME	-	-	18	98	30.1
Fiji	-	121	22	18	-	360	NO	YES	YES	YES	NO	-	-	90	45	-
Finland	-	182	7	4	Yes	8200	YES	YES	YES	YES	YES	-	Yes	176	-	26.9
France	-	168	9	5	-	2700	NO	NO	???	???	NO	Yes	Yes	157	-	32.7
Gabon	-	48	92	91	-	37	NO	YES	NO	NO	???	-	-	99	50	-
Gambia	Medium	27	151	137	-	31	NO	NO	YES	NO	NO	-	-	86	86	50.2
Georgia	-	72	47	45	No	1700	NO	YES	YES	YES	SOME	-	-	58	-	40.4
Germany	-	168	9	5	Yes	8000	YES	NO	YES	YES	YES	-	-	154	58	28.3
Ghana	Medium	42	122	112	-	35	NO	NO	YES	NO	NO	-	-	125	-	40.8
Greece	-	168	11	5	No	7100	YES	NO	YES	NO	YES	-	-	147	-	34.3
Grenada	-	108	37	21	-	-	NO	NO	SOME	NO	SOME	-	-	105	-	-

74 STATE OF THE WORLD'S STREET CHILDREN REPORT: **VIOLENCE**

Guatemala	High	73	82	43	-	74	NO	NO	YES	NO	NO	-	60	48	55.1
Guinea	Medium	21	240	150	-	18	NO	YES	[NO]	???	NO	-	9	96	40.3
Guinea-Bissau	-	12	253	200	-	13	NO	YES	YES	YES	???	-	38	92	47.0
Guyana	-	66	88	63	-	200	NO	NO	NO	NO	NO	-	99	-	-
Haiti	-	37	150	120	-	29	NO	YES	YES	YES	YES	-	11	74	59.2
Holy See	-	-	-	-	-	-	-	-	-	-	-	-	-	-	-
Honduras	High	76	59	40	Yes	190	NO	YES	YES	NO	NO	Yes	94	37	53.8
Hungary	-	154	17	8	Yes	4000	YES	YES	YES	YES	YES	-	139	-	26.9
Iceland	-	190	7	3	Yes	0	YES	YES	YES	YES	YES	-	171	-	-
India	High	54	123	74	No	48	NO	SOME	SOME	NO	NO	-	110	55	32.5
Indonesia	High	83	91	36	-	150	NO	NO	SOME	NO	NO	-	55	41	34.3
Iran (Islamic Republic of)	-	83	72	36	-	470	NO	YES	NO	NO	NO	-	57	35	43.0
Iraq	-	33	50	125	-	63	NO	YES	YES	???	???	-	2	-	-
Ireland	-	161	10	6	-	8300	NO	YES	YES	YES	SOME	-	174	-	34.3
Israel	Medium	161	12	6	Yes	1800	YES	YES	YES	YES	YES	-	75	-	39.2
Italy	-	182	9	4	Yes	13900	YES	YES	YES	YES	YES	-	156	-	36.0
Jamaica	High	113	20	20	-	380	NO	SOME	YES	YES	YES	Yes	123	30	37.9
Japan	-	182	6	4	Yes	6000	NO	YES	YES	YES	[SOME]	-	164	-	24.9
Jordan	Medium	100	40	26	-	450	NO	YES	YES	YES	[YES]	Yes	82	11	38.8
Kazakhstan	Medium	57	63	73	-	190	NO	SOME	YES	YES	SOME	-	103	-	33.9
Kenya	High	37	97	120	-	19	NO	YES	YES	YES	SOME	-	31	60	42.5
Kiribati	-	64	38	65	-	-	NO	YES	NO	NO	NO	-	-	-	-

Countries and Territories	Street Children Visibility Level 2006[7]	Child			Official Child Abuse and Neglect Counts (Child Abuse Register)[2]	Family		Corporal punishment of children prohibited in the home[3]	Corporal punishment of children prohibited in schools[3]	Corporal punishment of children prohibited in the penal system as sentence[3]	Corporal punishment of children prohibited in the penal system as disciplinary measure[3]	Corporal punishment of children prohibited in alternative care settings[3]	Community and Society			Failed States Index Rank 2007[5]	Human poverty index (HPI-1) Rank[6]	Gini Index[6]
		Under-5 mortality rank 2007[1]	Under-5 mortality rate 1990[1]	Under-5 mortality rate 2005[1]		Maternal mortality ratio, 2000	Lifetime risk of maternal death, 1 in:[1]						Countries with a national report on violence [and health][4]	Countries with a national policy document on violence[4]				
Korea, Dem People's Republic of	-	70	55	55	-	590	-	NO	NO	YES	YES	???	-	-	13	-	-
Korea, Republic of	-	168	9	5	Yes	2800	-	NO	NO	YES	YES	NO	-	-	152	-	31.6
Kuwait	-	146	16	11	-	6000	-	NO	YES	YES	NO	???	-	-	124	-	-
Kyrgyzstan	-	63	80	67	-	290	-	NO	NO	YES	YES	SOME	-	-	41	-	30.3
Lao People's Dem Republic	Medium	51	163	79	-	25	-	YES	YES	YES	YES	NO	-	-	44	63	34.6
Latvia	-	146	18	11	-	1800	-	NO	YES	YES	YES	YES	-	-	135	-	37.7
Lebanon	-	90	37	30	Yes	240	-	NO	NO	NO	NO	[SOME]	-	-	28	20	-
Lesotho	-	31	101	132	-	32	-	NO	NO	YES	NO	NO	-	-	62	89	63.2
Liberia	Medium	5	235	235	-	16	-	NO	YES	NO	???	???	-	-	27	-	-
Libyan Arab Jamahiriya	Low	117	41	19	-	240	-	NO	YES	YES	YES	SOME	-	-	115	-	-
Liechtenstein	-	182	10	4	-	-	-	NO	YES	YES	YES	YES	-	-	-	-	-
Lithuania	-	151	13	9	-	4900	-	NO	YES	YES	YES	NO	-	-	143	-	36.0
Luxembourg	-	168	10	5	-	1700	-	NO	NO	YES	???	SOME	-	-	165	-	-
Madagascar	-	40	168	119	-	26	-	NO	YES	YES	YES	NO	-	-	83	66	47.5
Malawi	Medium	33	221	125	-	7	-	NO	NO	YES	YES	SOME	-	-	29	83	50.3
Malaysia	Medium	140	22	12	Yes	660	-	NO	NO	NO	NO	NO	Yes	-	120	15	49.2

Maldives	-	74	111	42	-	140	NO	[YES]	NO	NO	SCME	-	-	66	36	-
Mali	Medium	7	250	218	-	10	NO	YES	YES	YES	NO	Yes	-	91	102	50.5
Malta	-	161	11	6	-	0	NO	YES	YES	YES	NO	-	-	144	-	-
Marshall Islands	-	69	92	58	-	-	NO	YES	YES	YES	NO	-	-	-	-	-
Mauritania	-	33	133	125	-	14	NO	NO	???	NO	NO	-	-	45	81	39.0
Mauritius	-	129	23	15	Yes	1700	NO	YES	YES	NO	NO	Yes	-	148	24	-
Mexico	High	96	46	27	Yes	370	NO	NO	YES	NO	NO	Yes	-	102	9	49.5
Micronesia (Federated States of)	-	74	58	42	-	-	NO	[YES]	YES	NO	NO	-	-	98	-	-
Moldova, Republic of	Low	128	35	16	-	1500	NO	YES	YES	YES	NO	-	-	48	-	33.2
Monaco	-	168	9	5	-	-	NO	NO	YES	YES	NO	-	-	-	-	-
Mongolia	Medium	71	108	49	Yes	300	NO	YES	YES	NO	NO	Yes	Yes	132	42	30.3
Montenegro‡	-	-	-	-	Yes	-	NO	YES	YES	YES	NO	-	-	136	-	-
Morocco	Medium	76	89	40	-	120	NO	NO	YES	NO	NO	Yes	-	86	59	39.5
Mozambique	-	24	235	145	-	14	NO	NO	YES	[NO]	NO	Yes	Yes	81	94	39.6
Myanmar	Medium	44	130	105	-	75	NO	NO	YES	NO	NO	-	-	14	47	-
Namibia	Medium	67	86	62	-	54	NO	YES	YES	YES	SOME	-	-	107	57	74.3
Nauru	-	90	-	30	-	-	NO	???	SOME	NO	???	-	-	-	-	-
Nepal	Medium	54	145	74	No	24	NO	NO	SOME	NO	NO	Yes	-	21	68	47.2
Netherlands	-	168	9	5	Yes	3500	YES	YES	YES	YES	YES	-	-	163	-	30.9
New Zealand	-	161	11	6	Yes	6000	YES	YES	YES	YES	YES	-	-	172	-	36.2
Nicaragua	High	82	68	37	-	88	NO	NO	YES	YES	NO	-	-	72	40	43.1
Niger	Medium	4	320	256	-	7	NO	NO	[YES]	[NO]	NO	-	-	32	99	50.5
Nigeria	Medium	14	230	194	-	18	NO	NO	SOME	[NO]	NO	-	-	17	76	43.7

Countries and Territories	Street Children Visibility Level 2006[7]	Child Under-5 mortality rank 2007[1]	Under-5 mortality rate 1990[1]	Under-5 mortality rate 2005[1]	Official Child Abuse and Neglect Counts (Child Abuse Register)?[2]	Family Maternal mortality ratio, 2000	Lifetime risk of maternal death, 1 in:[1]	Corporal punishment of children prohibited in the home[3]	Corporal punishment of children prohibited in schools[3]	Corporal punishment of children prohibited in the penal system as sentence[3]	Corporal punishment of children prohibited in the penal system as disciplinary measure[3]	Community and Society Corporal punishment of children prohibited in alternative care settings[3]	Countries with a national report on violence [and health][4]	Countries with a national policy document on violence[4]	Failed States Index Rank 2007[5]	Human poverty index (HPI-1) Rank[6]	Gini Index[6]
Niue	-	-	-	-	-	-	-	NO	???	YES	???	???	-	-	-	-	-
Norway	-	182	9	4	-	-	2900	YES	YES	YES	YES	YES	-	-	177	-	25.8
Occupied Palestinian Territory	-	106	40	23	-	-	-	NO	SOME	YES	NO	NO	-	-	-	8	-
Oman	Medium	140	32	12	-	-	140	NO	YES	???	NO	NO	-	-	146	-	-
Pakistan	Medium	47	130	99	No	-	170	NO	SOME	SOME	NO	NO	-	-	12	65	30.6
Palau	-	146	21	11	-	-	31	NO	YES	YES	NO	NO	-	-	-	-	-
Panama	-	103	34	24	-	-	-	NO	NO	YES	YES	NO	-	-	131	12	56.4
Papua New Guinea	-	54	94	74	-	-	210	NO	NO	YES	NO	NO	-	-	52	75	50.9
Paraguay	-	106	41	23	-	-	62	NO	NO	YES	YES	NO	-	-	101	14	57.8
Peru	Medium	96	78	27	No	-	120	NO	NO	NO	NO	SOME	-	-	85	25	54.6
Philippines	High	86	62	33	Yes	-	73	NO	YES	YES	YES	YES	-	-	56	31	46.1
Poland	-	156	18	7	No	-	120	NO	YES	YES	YES	NO	-	-	145	-	34.5
Portugal	-	168	14	5	No	-	4600	NO	NO	YES	YES	NO	-	-	162	-	38.5
Qatar	-	108	26	21	-	-	11100	NO	NO	NO	NO	NO	-	-	137	13	-
Romania	Medium	117	31	19	No	-	170	YES	YES	YES	YES	YES	-	-	126	-	31.0
Russian Federation	High	121	27	18	Yes	-	1300	NO	YES	YES	YES	NO	Yes	-	62	-	39.9

Rwanda	High	11	173	203	Yes	10	NO	NO	YES	YES	SOME	-	36	36	28.9
Saint Kitts and Nevis	-	113	36	20	-	-	NO	NO	NO	NO	NO	-	-	67	-
Saint Lucia	-	137	21	14	Yes	-	NO	NO	YES	NO	NO	-	-	-	-
Saint Vincent and the Grenadines	-	113	25	20	-	-	NO	NO	NO	NO	NO	-	-	-	-
Samoa	-	92	50	29	-	150	NO	NO	YES	[YES]	NO	-	97	-	-
San Marino	-	190	14	3	-	-	NO	YES	YES	YES	NO	-	-	-	-
Sao Tome and Principe	-	41	118	118	-	-	NO	[YES]	SOME	???	NO	-	77	-	-
Saudi Arabia	-	100	44	26	-	610	NO	NO	NO	NO	YES	-	83	-	-
Senegal	-	28	148	136	-	22	NO	YES	YES	SOME	NO	-	117	84	41.3
Serbia	-	-	-	-	No	-	NO	YES	YES	YES	NO	-	66	-	-
Seychelles	-	139	19	13	-	-	NO	NO	YES	[YES]	[YES]	-	107	-	-
Sierra Leone	High	1	302	282	-	6	NO	NO	NO	NO	NO	-	23	95	62.9
Singapore	-	190	9	3	Yes	1700	NO	NO	NO	NO	SOME	-	161	7	42.5
Slovakia	-	154	14	8	-	19800	NO	YES	YES	YES	YES	-	142	-	25.8
Slovenia	-	182	10	4	-	4100	NO	YES	YES	YES	SOME	-	155	-	28.4
Solomon Islands	-	92	38	29	-	120	NO	NO	YES	NO	NO	-	30	-	-
Somalia	-	6	225	225	No	10	NO	NO	YES	YES	NO	-	3	-	-
South Africa	High	61	60	68	Yes	120	NO	YES	YES	YES	YES	Yes	133	53	57.8
Spain	-	168	9	5	Yes	17400	NO	YES	YES	YES	NO	-	153	-	34.7
Sri Lanka	Medium	137	32	14	Yes	430	NO	NO	YES	YES	NO	Yes	25	38	33.2
Sudan	High	49	120	90	-	30	NO	NO	NO	NO	NO	-	1	54	-
Suriname	-	78	48	39	-	340	NO	NO	YES	YES	NO	-	96	23	-
Swaziland	-	20	110	160	-	49	NO	NO	NO	NO	NO	-	61	97	60.9

Countries and Territories	Street Children Visibility Level 2006[7]	Child			Family					Community and Society							
		Under-5 mortality rank 2007[1]	Under-5 mortality rate 1990[1]	Under-5 mortality rate 2005[1]	Official Child Abuse and Neglect Counts (Child Abuse Register)[2]	Maternal mortality ratio, 2000 Lifetime risk of maternal death, 1 in:[1]	Corporal punishment of children prohibited in the home[3]	Corporal punishment of children prohibited in schools[3]	Corporal punishment of children prohibited in the penal system as sentence[3]	Corporal punishment of children prohibited in the penal system as disciplinary measure[3]	Corporal punishment of children prohibited in alternative care settings[3]	Countries with a national report on violence (and health)[4]	Countries with a national policy document on violence[4]	Failed States Index Rank 2007[5]	Human poverty index (HPI-1) Rank[6]	Gini Index[6]
Sweden	-	182	7	4	No	29800	YES	YES	YES	YES	YES	-	-	175	-	25.0
Switzerland	-	168	9	5	-	7900	NO	YES	YES	YES	YES	-	-	173	-	33.7
Syrian Arab Republic	-	129	39	15	No	130	NO	NO	YES	???	NO	-	-	40	29	-
Tajikistan	-	59	115	71	Yes	250	NO	NO	YES	NO	NO	-	-	39	-	32.6
Tanzania, United Republic of	High	36	161	122	-	10	NO	NO	NO	NO	NO	-	-	76	64	34.6
Thailand	Medium	108	37	21	No	900	NO	YES	YES	YES	NO	Yes	-	86	19	42.0
The former Yugoslav Rep of Macedonia	-	125	38	17	-	2100	NO	YES	YES	YES	YES	Yes	Yes	95	-	39.0
Timor-Leste	Medium	68	177	61	-	30	NO	NO	YES	YES	NO	-	-	20	-	-
Togo	Medium	26	152	139	No	26	NO	NO	SOME	YES	NO	-	-	46	72	-
Tonga	-	103	32	24	-	-	NO	YES	NO	NO	NO	-	-	-	-	-
Trinidad and Tobago	-	117	33	19	-	330	NO	NO	YES	NO	NO	-	-	116	17	40.3
Tunisia	-	103	52	24	-	320	NO	NO	YES	YES	NO	-	-	122	39	39.8
Turkey	High	92	82	29	Yes	480	NO	YES	YES	YES	NO	-	-	92	21	43.6
Turkmenistan	-	45	97	104	No	790	NO	YES	YES	YES	???	-	-	43	-	40.8
Tuvalu	-	80	54	38	-	-	NO	NO	YES	NO	NO	-	-	-	-	-

Uganda	Medium	28	160	136	-	13	NO	NO	YES	YES	NO	-	-	15	62	43.0
Ukraine	High	125	26	17	-	2000	YES	YES	YES	YES	YES	-	-	106	-	28.1
United Arab Emirates	-	151	15	9	-	500	NO	YES	NO	NO	NO	-	-	138	34	-
United Kingdom	Low	161	10	6	Yes**	3800	NO	YES	YES	YES	SOME	Yes	-	157	-	36.0
United States	Low	156	12	7	Yes	2500	NO	SOME	YES	SOME	SOME	-	-	160	-	40.8
Uruguay	-	129	23	15	-	1300	NO	NO	YES	NO	NO	-	-	151	1	44.9
Uzbekistan	-	61	79	68	-	1300	NO	YES	YES	YES	NO	-	-	22	-	26.8
Vanuatu	-	80	62	38	-	140	NO	YES	SOME	[YES]	NO	-	-	-	49	-
Venezuela (Bolivarian Republic of)	High	108	33	21	-	300	NO	YES	YES	YES	NO	-	-	74	16	28.2
Viet Nam	High	117	53	19	-	270	NO	NO	YES	YES	NO	-	-	79	33	37.0
Yemen	-	46	139	102	No	19	NO	YES	NO	NO	NO	-	-	24	77	33.4
Zambia	-	18	180	182	No	19	NO	YES	YES	YES	NO	-	-	69	87	42.1
Zimbabwe	High	31	80	132	-	16	NO	NO	NO	NO	NO	-	-	4	88	50.1

*Including Hong Kong
**Information available for England and Scotland only.
1 UNICEF, (2006) *State of the World's Street Children 2007*. Reproduced with kind permission from UNICEF.
2 ISPCAN, (2006) *World Perspectives on Child Abuse: An International Resource Book Seventh Edition*. Reproduced with kind permission from ISPCAN.
3 Global summary of legal status of corporal punishment of children, September 2007 (info@endcorporalpunishment.org). Reproduced with kind permission of the Global Initiative to End All Corporal Punishment of Children.
4 WHO, (2007) *Third Milestones of a Global Campaign for Violence Prevention Report 2007: Scaling Up* Geneva: World Health Organization. Reproduced with kind permission from WHO.
5 UNICEF, (2006) *State of the World's Street Children 2007*. Reproduced with kind permission from The Fund for Peace.
6 UNDP, (2006) *Human Development Report 2006*. Reproduced with kind permission from Palgrave Macmillan.
7 Please see section 7.3.2 for further information on how this column has been compiled.

References

Abdelgalil, S., Gurgel, R.G., Theobald, S. and Cuevas, L.E., (2004) "Household and Family Characteristics of Street Children in Aracaju, Brazil." *Archives in Disease of Childhood*, 89(9): 817-20.

Aber, J.L., Jones, S., Brown, J., Chaudry, N. and Samples, F., (1998) "Resolving Conflict Creatively: Evaluating the Developmental Effects of a School-Based Violence Prevention Program in Neighborhood and Classroom Context." *Development and Psychopathology*, 10: 187–213.

Ainsworth, M.D.S., Blehar, M., Waters, E. and Wall, (1978) *Patterns of Attachment: A Psychological Study of the Strange Situation*. Hillsdale, NJ: Erlbaum.

Ali, M. and de Muynck, A., (2005) "Illness Incidence and Health Seeking Behaviour Among Street Children in Rawalpindi and Islamabad, Pakistan - a Qualitative Study." *Child: Care, Health and Development*, 31(5): 525–532.

Aptekar, L., (2004) "The Changing Developmental Dynamics of Children in Particularly Difficult Circumstances: Examples of Street and War-Traumatized Children" in Gielen, U. and Roopnarine, J. (Eds.) *Childhood and Adolescence: Cross-Cultural Perspectives and Applications* (pp. 377-410). Westport, Conneticut: Praeger Publishers/Greenwood Publishing Group.

Aptekar, L. and Heinonen, P., (2003) "Methodological Implications of Contextual Diversity in Research on Street Children." *Children, Youth and Environments,* 13(1). Retrieved 31 June 2007 from http://www.colorado.edu/journals/cye.

Ayuku, D., Kaplan, C., Baar, H. and de Vries, M., (2004) "Characteristics and Personal Social Networks of the On-the-Street, Off-the-Street, Shelter and School Children in Eldoret, Kenya." *International Social Work,* 47(3): 293-311.

Azar, S., Robinson, D., Hekimian, E. and Twentyman, C., (1984) "Unrealistic Expectations and Problem-Solving Ability in Maltreating and Comparison Mothers." *Journal of Consulting and Clinical Psychology,* 52: 687-691.

Bandura, A., (1975) *Social Learning Theory*. New Jersey: Prentice Hall.

Bar-On, A., (1997) "Criminalising Survival: Images and Reality of Street Children." *Journal of Social Policy*, 26(1): 63-78.

Barker, G., (2000) *What about Boys? A Literature Review on the Health and Development of Adolescent Boys*. Geneva: WHO.

Barker, G., (2005) *Dying to be Men - Youth, Masculinity and Social Exclusion*. Routledge: London.

Barker, G., and Knaul, F. with Cassaniga, N. and Schrader, A., (2000) *Urban Girls: Empowerment in Especially Difficult Circumstances*. London: Intermediate Technology Publications.

Batmanghelidjh, C., (2006) *Shattered Lives: Children who Live with Courage and Dignity*. London: Jessica Kingsley Publishers.

Baumrind, D., (1994) "The Social Context of Child Maltreatment." *Family Relations*, 43(4): 360-368.

Beazley, H., (2003) "The Construction and Protection of Individual and Collective Identities by Street Children and Youth in Indonesia." *Children, Youth and Environments*, 13(1).

Belsky, J., (1993) "Etiology of Child Maltreatment: A Developmental-Ecological Analysis" *Psychological Bulletin*, 114: 413-34.

Black, M., (1993) *Street and Working Children: Global Seminar Report*. Florence: UNICEF.

Black, D., Schumacher, J., Smith Slep, A. and Heyman, R., (1999) *Risk Factors for Partner Abuse and Child Maltreatment: A Review of Literature*. C.M. Allen (Ed.). Retrieved 31 June 2004 from http://www.nnh.org/risk.

Bowlby, J., (1969) *Attachment and Loss, Vol. 1: Attachment*. London: Hogarth Press.

Bray, R., (2003) *Predicting The Social Consequences Of Orphanhood In South Africa CSSR Working Paper No. 29*. Centre for Social Science Research University of Cape Town.

Bronfenbronner, U., (1979) *The Ecology Of Human Development: Experiments by Nature and Design*. Cambridge, Ma: Harvard University Press.

Burchardt, T., Le Grand, J. and Piachaud, D., (2002) "Introduction to Understanding Social Exclusion" in Hills, J., Le Grand, J. and Piachaud, D. (Eds.) *Understanding Social Exclusion*. Oxford: Oxford University Press.

Burgess, R. and Garbarino, J., (1983) "Doing What Comes Naturally? An Evolutionary Perspective on Child Abuse" in Finkelhor, D., Gelles, R., Hotaling, G. and Straus, M. (Eds.), *The Dark Side of Families*. Newbury Park, CA: Sage.

Burr, R., (2006) *Vietnam's Children in a Changing World*. Rutgers University Press.

Butler, U. and Rizzini, I. (2003) "Young People Living and Working on the Streets of Brazil: Revisiting the Literature." *Children, Youth and Environments* 13(1). Retrieved May 2006 from http://colorado.edu/journals/cye.

Caliso, J. and Milner, J., (1994) "Childhood Physical Abuse, Childhood Social Support, and Adult Child Abuse Potential." *Journal of Interpersonal Violence*, 9(1): 27-44.

CENDIF (Centro de Investigaciones para La Infancia y La Familia), (1999) *Interacción Temprana Mamá-Bebé*. Caracas: Cendif-Unimet.

COESNICA, (1992) "I Street Children Study, Executive Summary: Mexico City." *Commission for the Study of Street Children,* Mexico City: UNICEF/DIF.

COESNICA, (1996) "II Street Children Study, Executive Summary: Mexico City." *Commission for the Study of Street Children,* Mexico City: UNICEF/DIF.

Coleman, J.S., (1988) "Social Capital in the Creation of Human Capital." *American Journal of Sociology,* 94(Supplement): S95-S120.

Conticini, A. and Hulme, D., (2006) "Escaping Violence, Seeking Freedom: Why Children In Bangladesh Migrate To The Street." Global Poverty Research Group, *Working Paper Series: 047*.

Coohey,C., (1996) "Child Maltreatment: Testing the Social Isolation Hypothesis." *Child Abuse and Neglect,* 20(3): 241-54.

CRC, (2005) "Committee on the Rights of the Child - Concluding Observations." Retrieved 30 May 2006 from http://www1.umn.edu/humanrts/crc/togo2005b.html.

Cyrulnik, B. and Fairfield, S., (2005) *The Whispering of Ghosts: Trauma and Resilience*. New York, NY, US: Other Press.

Dorning, K., (2002) *World Vision Myanmar Street Children Centres*. Yangon: World Vision Myanmar.

Dowdney, L., (2003) *Children of the Drug Trade: A Case Study of Children in Organized Armed Violence in Rio de Janeiro*. Rio de Janeiro, Brazil: 7 Letras.

Downing-Orr, K., (1999) *Alienation and Social Support: A Social Psychological Study of Homeless Young People in London and Sydney*. Aldershot: Averbury.

Dynamo, (2005) *Social Street Work and Communication with the Media*. Brussels: Dynamo. Retrieved 15 June 2007 from http://www.travail-de-rue.net.

Droz, Y., (2006) "Street Children And The Work Ethic: New Policy for an Old Moral, Nairobi (Kenya)." *Childhood: A Global Journal of Child Research,* 13(3): 349-363.

Durrant, J., (2007) *Positive Discipline: What it is and how to do it*. Thailand: Save the Children Sweden Southeast Asia and the Pacific.

Dunst, C.J. and Trivette, C.M., (1990) "Assessment of Social Support in Early Intervention Programs" in Meisels, S.J. and Shonkoff, J.P. (Eds.) *Handbook of Early Childhood Intervention*. New York, Cambridge University Press.

Ennew, J., (2000) "Why the Convention is not about Street Children" in Fottrell, D. (Ed.) *Revisiting Children's Rights: 10 Years of the UN Convention on the Rights of the Child*. The Hague: Kluwer Law International.

Ennew, J., (1994) "Parentless Friends: A Cross-Cultural Examination of Networks Amongst Street Children and Youth" in Nestmann, F. and Hurrelmann, K. (Eds.) *Social Networks and Social Support in Childhood and Adolescence*. Berlin and New York: Walter de Gruyter.

Ennew, J. and Milne, B., (1989) *The Next Generation: Lives of Third World Children*. London: Zed Books.

Evans, R., (2006) "Negotiating Social Identities: The Influence of Gender, Age and Ethnicity on Young People's 'Street Careers' in Tanzania." *Children's Geographies*, 4(1): 109.

Feeny, T., (2005) *In Best or Vested interests? An Exploration of the Concept and Practice of Family Reunification for Street Children*. London: Consortium for Street Children.

Ferguson, K., (2005) "Child Labor and Social Capital in the Mezzosystem: Family- and Community-Based Risk and Protective Factors for Street-Working Children in Mexico." *Journal of Social Work Research and Evaluation,* 6(1): 101-120.

Fonagy, P., Steele, M., Steele, H., Leigh, T., Kennedy, R., Mattoon, G. and Target, M., (1995) "Attachment, the Reflective Self, and Borderline States: The Predictive Specificity of the Adult Attachment Interview and Pathological Emotional Development" in Goldberg, S. and Kerr, J. (Eds.) *Attachment Research: The State of the Art* (pp. 233-77). Hillsdale, NJ: Analytic.

Garbarino, J. and Kostelny, K., (1993) "Neighbourhood and Community Influences on Parenting" in Luster, T. and Okagaki, L. (Eds.) *Parenting: An Ecological Perspective*. Hillsdale, NJ: Lawrence Erlbaum Associates.

Glauser, B., (1990) "Street Children: Deconstructing a Construct" in James, A. and Prout, A. (Eds.) *Constructing and Reconstructing Childhood: Contemporary Issues in the Sociological Study of Childhood* (pp. 138-56). London-Falmer.

Graham, B., Tanner, G., Cheyne, B., Freeman, I., Rooney, M. and Lambie, A., (1998) "Unemployment Rates, Single Parent Density, and Indices of Child Poverty: Their Relationship to Different Categories of Child Abuse and Neglect." *Child Abuse and Neglect*, 22(2): 79-90.

Green, D., (1998) *Hidden Lives: Voices of Children in Latin America and the Caribbean*. London: Cassell.

Gregorian, R. and Hura-Tudor, E. with Feeny, T., (2003) *Street Children and Juvenile Justice in Romania*. Asociatia Sprijinirea Integrarii Sociale (ASIS)/Consortium for Street Children, London.

Gutierrez, R. and Vega, L., (2003) "Las investigaciones psicosociales sobre la subsistencia infantil en las calles desarrolladas en el INP durante los ultimos 25 anos" ["Psychosocial Research on Street Living Children Developed by the INP During the Last 25 Years", Spanish]. *Salud Mental,* 26(6): 27-34.

Hashima, P. and Amato, P., (1994) "Poverty, Social Support And Parental Behaviour." *Child Development*, 65: 394-403.

Hecht, T., (1998) *At Home in the Street: Street Children of Northeast Brazil*. Cambridge, UK: Cambridge University Press.

Herrera, E., Jones, G. and Thomas de Benítez, S., (2008) "Bodies on the Line: Identity Markers Among Mexican Street Youth" in *Children's Geographies,* Special Issue on 'Contested Bodies' (forthcoming).

Holmes, J., (1996) "Attachment Theory: A Secure Base for Policy?" in Kraemer, S. and Roberts, J. (Eds.) *The Politics of Attachment: Towards a Secure Society* (pp. 27-42). London: Free Association Books.

Howe, D., Brandon, M., Hinnigs, D. and Schofield, G., (1999) *Attachment Theory, Child Development and Family Support: a Practice and Assessment Model.* Basingstoke: Macmillan

Huang, C., Barreda, P., Mendonza, V., Guzman, L. and Gilbert, P., (2004) "A Comparative Analysis of Abandoned Street Children and Formerly Abandoned Street Children in La Paz, Bolivia." *Archives of Disease in Children*; 89(9): 821-6.

Human Rights Watch, (2001*) Easy Targets: Violence Against Children Worldwide.* Retrieved 25 May 2007 from http://www.hrw.org/reports/2001/children/children.pdf.

Human Rights Watch, (2002) *My Gun is as Tall as Me: Child Soldiers in Burma.* New York: Human Rights Watch.

Human Rights Watch, (2003a) *Borderline Slavery: Child Trafficking in Togo*. Retrieved 30 May 2007 from http://www.hrw.org/reports/2003/togo0403.

Human Rights Watch, (2003b) *Rwanda Lasting Wounds: Consequences of Genocide and War on Rwanda's Children*. Vol. 15:5.

Human Rights Watch, (2006) *What Future? Street Children in the Democratic Republic of Congo*. Vol. 18:2(A).

Hussein, N., (2005) *Street Children in Egypt: Group Dynamics & Subculture Constituents.* Cairo: The American University in Cairo Press.

IPU-UNICEF, (2007) *Eliminating Violence against Children: a Parliamentary Handbook.* New York: UNICEF.

ISPCAN, (2006) *World Perspectives on Child Abuse: An International Resource Book Seventh Edition.* Chicago, IL: International Society for Prevention of Child Abuse and Neglect.

Jack, G., (2001) "An Ecological Perspective on Child Abuse" in Foley, P., Roche, J. and Tucker, S. (Eds.) *Children in Society: Contemporary Theory, Policy and Practice.* Basingstoke: Palgrave.

Jones, G., Herrera, E. and Thomas de Benítez, S., (2007) "Tears, Trauma and Suicide: Everyday Violence Among Street Youth in Puebla, Mexico." *Bulletin of Latin American Research*, 26(4): 462–479.

Kidd, S., (2007) "Youth Homelessness and Social Stigma." *Journal of Youth and Adolescence,* 36: 291–299.

Lee, J. and Odie-Alie, S (2000) "Carry Me Home: A Collaborative Study of Street Children in Georgetown, Guyana." *Journal of Social Work Research and Evaluation,* 1(2): 185-196.

Lloyd, S., (2006) *Guatemala Country Paper.* Internal document prepared for the State of the World's Street Children: Violence report.

Lucchini, R., (1997) *Deviance and Street Children in Latin America: the Limits of a Functionalist Approach.* Fribourg, Switzerland: University of Fribourg Press.

Lucchini, R., (1996) *Sociologie de la Survie: L'enfant dans la Rue.* Paris: PUF.

Lucchini, R., (1999) *Niño de la calle: Identidad, Sociabilidad, Droga* [Spanish]. Barcelona: Libros de la Frontera.

Luthar, S., (2006) "Resilience in Development: A Synthesis of Research Across Five Decades" in Cicchetti, D. and Cohen, D. (Eds.) *Developmental Psychopathology: Risk, Disorder, and Adaptation* (pp. 739-795). New York, NY: John Wiley and Sons.

Mikulak, M., (2003) "The Social Construction of Disposable Children: Street and Working Children in Curvelo, Minas Gerais, Brazil." *Dissertation Abstracts International,* Section A: Humanities and Social Sciences, 63(11-A): 3994.

Moura, S., (2002) "The Social Construction of Street Children: Configuration and Implications." *British Journal of Social Work,* 32: 353-367.

National Research Council, (1993) *Understanding Child Abuse and Neglect.* Washington DC: National Academy of Sciences Press.

Newell, P., (2000) *Taking Children Seriously – a Proposal for a Children's Rights Commissioner.* London: Calouste Gulbenkian Foundation.

Newman, T. and Blackburn, S., (2002) *Transitions in the Lives of Children and Young People: Resilience Factors.* Edinburgh: Scottish Executive Education Department.

Norwegian Government, (1995) *Summary of the Norwegian Parliament Committee's Conclusions from the Norwegian Official Report 'The Commissioner for Children, and Childhood in Norway'.* NOU: 26.

Ordoñez, D., (1996) *Niños de la calle y sus familias en Lima: una realidad en 852 variables* [Spanish]. Vols. 1 & 2. Lima: AYNI.

Panter-Brick, C., (2002) "Street Children, Human Rights, and Public Health: A Critique and Future Directions." *Annual Review Anthropology,* 31:147–171.

Parr, M., (2003) *Underpinning Theories and Principles.* PIPPIN (Parents in Partnership Parent Infant Network) Training Manual.

Pinheiro, P., (2006) *World Report on Violence against Children.* New York: United Nations Secretary General's Study on Violence against Children.

Plan, (2005) *For the Price of a Bike: Child Trafficking in Togo*. Retrieved 29 May 2006 from http://www.plan-international.org/pdfs/togoreport.

Portes, A., (1998) "Social Capital: Its Origins and Applications in Modern Sociology." *Annual Review of Sociology,* 24(1): 1-24.

Raffaelli, M., (1999) "Homeless and Working Street Youth in Latin America: A Developmental Review." *Interamerican Journal of Pyschology,* 33(2): 7-28.

Raffaelli, M., (2000) "Gender Differences In Brazilian Street Youth's Family Circumstances and Experiences on the Street." *Child Abuse & Neglect,* 24(11): 1431-41.

Railway Children, (2006) *Girls on the Street.* Unpublished Report, India: The Railway Children.

Rede Rio Criança, (2007) *Criança, Rua e ONG's: Quem Faz e o que faz? Mapeamento de Ações das ONG's Junto às Crianças e Adolescentes em Situação de Rua no Município do RJ.* Rio de Janeiro: Criação Gráfica.

Rees, G. and Lee, J., (2005) *Still Running II.* London: The Children's Society.

Ringwalt, C., Greene, J. and Robertson, M., (1998) "Familial Backgrounds and Risk Behaviors of Youth with Throwaway Experiences." *Journal of Adolescence,* 21: 241–252.

Rizzini, I., (1996) "Street Children: An Excluded Generation in Latin America." *Childhood: A Global Journal of Child Research,* 3(2): 215-233.

Rizzini, I. and Butler, U., (2003) "Life Trajectories of Children and Adolescents Living on the Streets of Rio de Janeiro." *Children, Youth and Environments,* 13(1).

Runyan, D., Hunter, M., Socolar, R., Amaya-Jackson, L., English, D., Landsverk, J., Dubowitz, H., Browne, D., Bandigwala, S. and Mathew, R., (1998) "Children Who Prosper in Unfavorable Environments: The Relationship to Social Capital." *Pediatrics,* 101(1): 12-20.

Rutter, M., (2006) "Implications of Resilience Concepts for Scientific Understanding." *Resilience in Children,* 1094: 1–12.

Scheper-Hughes, N., (2004) "Dangerous and Endangered Youth: Social Structures and Determinants of Violence." *Annals of the New York Academy of Sciences,* 1036(1): 13–46.

Schrader, A., (2005) *Circles of Trust: Parent Education and the Reversal of Child Maltreatment in Post-War Guatemala.* Unpublished PhD Thesis: Liverpool University.

Schrader, A. and Veale, A., (1999) *Resource Pack: Prevention of Street Migration.* London: Consortium for Street Children and University College Cork.

Sen, A., (1992) *Inequality Reexamined.* Oxford: Clarendon Press.

Sherman, S., Plitt, S., ul Hassan, S., Cheng, Y. and Zafar, S., (2005) "Drug Use, Street Survival, and Risk Behaviour Among Street Children in Lahore, Pakistan." *Journal of Urban Health,* 82(3), Suppl 4: 113-24.

Shonkoff, J. and Phillips, D. (Eds.), (2000) *From Neurons to Neighbourhoods: The Science of Early Childhood Development.* Washington DC: National Academy Press.

Smeaton, E., (2005) *Living on the Edge: The Experiences of Detached Young Runaways*. London: The Children's Society.

Staller, K., (2004) "Youth System Dynamics: A Theoretical Framework for Analyzing Runaway and Homeless Youth Policy." *Families in Society*, 85(3): 379-390.

Stephenson, S., (2001) "Street Children in Moscow: Using and Creating Social Capital." *The Sociological Review*, 49(4): 530-547.

Straus, M., (1994) *Beating the Devil Out of Them: Corporal Punishment in American Families*. New York: Lexington Books.

Tan, G., Ray, M. and Cate, R., (1991) "Migrant Farm Child Abuse and Neglect within an Ecosystem Framework." *Family Relations,* 40(1): 84-90.

Tari, I. and Ziyalar, N., (2005) "Comparing Street Children Who Use Inhalant in Terms of Suicide Attempt" ["İntihar Girişimi Olan Ve Olmayan Sokakta Yaşayan Uçucu Madde Kullanıcılarının Karşılaştırılması", Turkish]. *Bağımlılık Dergisi,* 6(2): 84-88.

The African Child Policy Forum, (2006) *Born to High Risk: Violence against Girls in Africa*. Retrieved August 2007 from http://www.africanchildforum.org.

Thomas de Benítez, S., (2001) *What Works in Street Children Programming: The JUCONI Model*. Baltimore: International Youth Foundation.

Thomas de Benítez, S., [ed.] (1999) *Creando Soluciones para Niños en Situación de Calle* [*Creating Solutions for Children in Street Situations*, Spanish]. Mexico: META-UNESCO.

Tomison, A., (1996) "Intergenerational Transmission of Maltreatment." *Issues in Child Abuse Prevention,* National Child Protection Clearing house. Issues Paper Number 6.

Tomison, A. and Wise, S., (1999) "'Community-Based Approaches in Preventing Child Maltreatment." *Issues in Child Abuse Prevention*, Number 11. Melbourne: National Child Protection Clearinghouse, Australian Institute of Family Studies.

Tyler, K. and Cauce, Ai., (2000) "Perpetrators of Early Physical and Sexual Abuse Among Homeless and Runaway Adolescents." *Child Abuse & Neglect,* 26(12): 1261-1274.

UNESCO, (2007) *Strong Foundations: Early Childhood Care and Education*. EFA Global Monitoring Report. Paris: UNESCO.

UNICEF, (2002) *State of the World's Children 2003*. New York: UNICEF.

UNICEF, (2005) *State of the World's Children 2006: Excluded and Invisible*. New York: UNICEF.

UNICEF, (2006) *State of the World's Children 2007: Women and Children*. New York: UNICEF.

UNICEF, (2007) *Child Poverty in Perspective: An Overview of Child Well-Being in Rich Countries*. Innocenti Report Card 7. UNICEF Innocenti Research Centre, Florence.

UNDP, (2006) *Human Development Report 2006: 'Beyond Scarcity: Power, Poverty and the Global Water Crisis'*. New York: Palgrave Macmillan.

UN OCHA, (2007) *Youth in crisis: Coming of age in the 21st century*. IRIN News and Analysis, February 2007, UN Office for the Coordination of Humanitarian Affairs. Retrieved 16 June 2007 from http://www.irinnews.org/pdf/in-depth/Youth-in-crisis-IRIN-In-Depth.pdf.

US State Department, (2006) *Trafficking in Persons Report*. Retrieved 7 June 2006 from http://www.state.gov/g/tip/rls/tiprpt/2006/index.htm.

Van Blerk, L., (2005) "Negotiating Spatial Identities: Mobile Perspectives on Street Life in Uganda." *Children's Geographies*, 3(1): 5-21.

Van Bueren, G., (2007) "Legal Opinion: Governments' Obligations to Girls - The Status and Effects of Article 2 of the Convention on the Rights of the Child 1989" in *Because I am a Girl: The State of the World's Girls 2007* (pp. 19-21). London: Plan UK.

Veale, A., Taylor, M. and Linehan, C., (2000) "Psychological Perspectives of 'Abandoned' and 'Abandoning' Street Children" in Panter-Brick, C. and Smith, M. (Eds.) *Abandoned Children* (pp. 131-145). Cambridge UK: Cambridge University Press.

Wernham, M., (2004) *An Outside Chance: Street Children and Juvenile Justice – an International Perspective*. London: Consortium for Street Children.

Whipple, E. and Webster-Stratton, C., (1991) "The Role of Parental Stress in Physically Abusive Families." *Child Abuse & Neglect,* 15: 279-291.

Wilkinson, R., (1996) *Unhealthy Societies: The Afflictions of Inequality*. London: Routledge.

World Bank, (2006) *World Development Report 2007: Development and the Next Generation*. Washington DC: World Bank.

WHO, (2002) *World Report on Violence and Health*. Geneva: World Health Organization.

WHO, (2007) *Third Milestones of a Global Campaign for Violence Prevention Report 2007: Scaling Up*. Geneva: World Health Organization.

WMA, (2003) *The World Medical Association Statement On Violence And Health*. Adopted By The WMA General Assembly, Helsinki. Retrieved from http://www.wma.net/e/policy.

Young, L., (2004) "Journeys to the Street: The Complex Migration Geographies of Ugandan Street Children." *Geoforum*, 35(4): 471-488.

Case Study Footnotes

Case Study 1: Street Children in Bangladesh
1. US State Department 2005, quoting a 2002 report by Government news agency Bangladesh Shongbad Shongsta [http://www.state.gov/g/drl/rls/hrrpt/2004/41738.htm].
2. [http://www.state.gov/g/drl/rls/hrrpt/2004/41738.htm]
3. [http://www.globalmarch.org/resourcecentre/world/bangladesh.pdf]
4. For general information about Sexual abuse and exploitation of children in Bangladesh see: [http://www.unicef.org/bangladesh/Child_Abuse_Exploitation_and_Trafficking.pdf].
5. NGOs known to work specifically with child groups in Dhaka City are: Nari Moitree (in Kamalapur railways station on awareness about Sexually Transmitted Infections); Incidin Bangladesh (through a day shelter, food and counseling in the commercial area of Shantinagar); CARE Bangladesh (providing condoms and raising awareness).
6. The results of the research and the details of the phases of the project can be found in Aparajeyo's publication: *"There is hope, An Action Based Research – Children Victims of sexual abuse and exploitation"*, Aparajeyo-Bangladesh, 2005, Dhaka.

Case Study 2: Street Children in Cambodia
7. Save the Children New Zealand. 'What we do and why: Cambodia'. [http://www.savethechildren.net/new_zealand/what_we_do/our_projects/cambodia.html] [accessed 01/05/07]; Mith Samlanh/Friends, (2001) 'Survey on Substance Use Among Street Children in Phnom Penh' [http://www.streetfriends.org/CONTENT/ABOUT_US/drugsurvey.pdf].
8. UNESCO, (Bangkok) 'Cambodia'. [http://www.unescobkk.org/index.php?id=3370].
9. World Vision, (2001) 'Children's Work, Adult's Play: Child Sex Tourism – the Problem in Cambodia'. [http://www.worldvision.com.au/resources/files/children%27s%20work%20adults%27%20play.pdf].
10. APLE, a NGO specializing in legal support including monitoring child sexual abuse.
11. ChildSafe (CS) is a programme created by M'Lop Tapang's partner in Phnom Penh - Friends International.

Case Study 4: Street Children and Reconciliation in Sierra Leone
12. HDR 2006 – Sierra Leone ranks 176 in the world - 2nd from bottom ranked Niger – in terms of its human development.
13. UNICEF, (2007) *State of the World's Children*, p. 110.
14. UN data on Sierra Leone [http://www.un.org/works/beijing+10/sierraleone.html].
15. UNICEF 'Sierra Leone at a glance', [http://www.unicef.org/infobycountry/sierraleone_34552.html] and UN 'Action to assist war-affected children in Sierra Leone proposed by special representative for children and armed conflict' [http://www.un.org/children/conflict/pr/1999-09-14actiontoassistwa78.html].
16. Amnesty International, 'Sierra Leone, Childhood – a casualty of conflict' [http://web.amnesty.org/library/Index/engAFR510692000]. Human Rights Watch, (2003) report *'We'll Kill You if You Cry: Sexual Violence in the Sierra Leone Conflict'* esti mates that as many as 257,000 Sierra Leonean women and girls were raped during the civil war [http://hrw.org/reports/2003/sierraleone/]. Women War Peace estimated that a number as high as a quarter of a million women have been raped during the conflict [http://www.womenwarpeace.org/sierra_leone/sierra_leone.htm].
17. This despite a key article of the final agreement calling for special attention to be paid to victimized women and girls in formulating and implementing rehabilitation, reconstruction and development programmes (Mazurana, D., and Carlson, K., (2004) *'From Combat to Community: Women and Girls of Sierra Leone'*, Women Waging Peace, Cambridge, Massachusetts & Washington, D.C. January, p.16).
18. Numbers are contested: 1,225 street children were registered in October 2004 (Ministry of Social Welfare, Gender and Children's Affairs, 3rd data collection), but the NGO community and media reports estimate much higher numbers.
19. A very positive independent external evaluation was undertaken in April 2007 and shows the success achieved in the first three years. A second stage of the project is in the process of being implemented.

Case Study 5: Street Children and Community Schools in Ecuador
20. UK-based NGO International Children's Trust and JUCONI Ecuador: 'Building Bridges Project' funded by the European Commission and Big Lottery.
21. The Social Contract for Education, (2004) II Consultation of children and adolescents first edition Quito Ecuador.
22. The Social Contract for Education, (2004) 'Workbooks from the Social Contract for Education' #2, September, First edition Quito Ecuador.
23. JUCONI Ecuador, (2006) Systematization of focus groups' report 'How my school is progressing' held with children from the schools participating in International Children's Trust - JUCONI Ecuador project.

Case Study 6: Street Children and Drugs in Salvador, Brazil
24. Procópio, A., (1999) *O Brasil no Mundo das Drogas*. Petrópolis: Editora Vozes.
25. Ibid.
26. Brazil has one of the highest levels of income inequality in the world: see UNDP, (2006) *Human Development Report* New York : Palgrave McMillan.
27. The economic crisis of the 1980s led to soaring unemployment rates. See Dantas, F., (2000) *"Crises empurraram adolescentes para o crime."* O Estado de São Paulo newspaper, July 9th, 2000.

28. UNICEF Brazil, (1993) *Brazil: Situation Analysis, Country Programme 1994-2000 'Children and Adolescents; Right to have Rights'*, Sao Paulo: UNICEF.
29. Uchôa, M.A., (1996) *Crack: O Caminho das Pedras,* São Paulo: Editora Ática.
30. Dimenstein, G., (1991) *Brazil: War on Children*. London: Latin American Bureau; and Raphael, A., and Berkman, J., (1992) *Children Without a Future*. Washington, D.C.: Brazil Network.

Case Study 7: Street Children and State-sponsored Police Violence in Uganda
31. Research information provided by 180 Degrees Global Alliance for Street children. Names of NGOs involved are not provided for their own safety and protection [www.180degreesalliance.org].
32. BBC News, 21st February 2007, [http://news.bbc.co.uk/2/hi/africa/6378969.stm].

Case Study 8: Street Children and Police in Guatemala
33. See US Department of State Country Reports on Human Rights Practices, 2006.
34. Ibid.

Case Study 10: Street Children and Public Stigmatization: Egypt
35. UNICEF, (2006) A new approach to Egypt's street children [www.unicef.org/infobycountry/egypt] [accessed 07 July 2007].
36. Ibid.
37. Hussein, N., (2005) *Street Children in Egypt: Group Dynamics & Subculture Constituents* (Cairo; The American University in Cairo Press) p.5.
38. Human Rights Watch, (2003) *Charged With Being Children: Egyptian Police Abuse of Children in Need of Protection* (New York; Human Rights Watch), p.39.
39. bid, p.3.
40. CRC Coalition, (2000) *NGOs Report on the Rights of the Child in Egypt*. (Cairo; Attala Publishing House), p. 25.

Case Study 11: Street Children and Detention in Kyrgyzstan
41. Not his real name
42. Organization for Security and Cooperation in Europe (OSCE)

Case Study 12: Street Children and Protection in Care in Mexico
43. Also known as 'double deprivation'. For a description see Williams, G., (1997) *Internal Landscapes and Foreign Bodies*, Duckworth.
44. Considerable evidence supports the maxim 'unhealed trauma will repeat itself N number of times'. See Zulueta, F., (1993) *From Pain to Violence: The Traumatic Roots of Destructiveness*. Whurr Publishers Ltd.
45. Developed from Steve de Shazer´s work on Solution-Focused Brief Therapy [www.brief-therapy.org] and Lee and Marlene Canter's ideas on Assertive Discipline [www.behaviouradvisor.com/AssertiveDiscipline].
46. Juconi adopted the "Safety Plan" among many other ideas, from the Sanctuary Model developed by Dr. Sandra Bloom and colleagues [www.sanctuaryweb.com].

Case Study 13: Street Children and the Law in Tanzania
47. Chapter 104 of the Laws of Tanganyika.
48. The Citizen Newspaper, 13 April, 2005.
49. Arusha Times Newspaper, 17-23 April, 2004.
50. Arusha Caucus for Children's Rights, 2005 Position paper: Police round-ups of street children in Arusha are unjust, inhumane and unconstitutional.
51. Feuerbach stated this idea in the following principle: "Nulla poena sine culpa" (No punishment without guilt).
52. United Nations Convention on the Rights of the Child (CRC)
53. African Charter on the Rights and Welfare of the Child (ACRWC)
54. United Nations International Covenant on Civil and Political Rights (ICCPR)
55. In May 2005, Mkombozi identified 21 children imprisoned in Kisongo adult jail.
56. Information obtained by Mkombozi social workers during interviews with rounded up street children on 5 September, 2005.
57. The right of not being denied rights to which a person in entitled by Domestic and International legislation.

Case Study 14: Street Children and Structural Violence in Latin America
58. Pinheiro, S., (2006) *World Report on Violence against Children*, UN.

Case Study 15: Street Children in Countries in Crisis: Iraq
59. See for example Wencke Aamodt Lind's article 'Experience from capacity-building courses for social workers in Iraq' *International Social Work* 50(3): 395–404 Sage Publications: London.
60. *Acutely Marginalised Children in Southern Iraq,* War Child, 2007.
61. Figures from Iraq's Ministry of Education indicate only 30% of Iraq's 3.5 million students are attending school (cited in O'Malley, B., (2007) *'Education under attack: A global study on targeted political and military violence against education staff, students, teachers, union and government officials, and educational institutions'* UNESCO: Paris).

Case Study 16: Street Children and Natural Disasters: Sri Lanka
62. WWW Virtual Library Sri Lanka: (http://www.lankalibrary.com/news.html).

About the Photographers

Pep Bonet
Born 1974 in Majorca, Pep moved at 15 to Andalusia to practice windsurfing which took him to the 1995 world championships. Two years later he moved to Amsterdam and studied photography, taking it up professionally after being inspired by an Ed Van Der Elsken exhibition.

Pep has won many prizes and awards. These include selection for the World Press Photo Master Class for his work Faith from Sierra Leone (2002) and by Photoespaña for his Procession of San Lazaro in Cuba (2002), as well as Kodak Young Photographer of the Year (2003). Nominated best press photographer of the year by the Luchetta Foundation in Trieste (2004), Pep won the W.Eugene Smith Award for Humanitarian Photography in 2005. In 2007 Pep won second prize in the World Press Photo in Sports for work on the amputees' football league in Sierra Leone.

Pep's books include: HIV/AIDS - VIH/SIDA (Rozenburg, 2005).

Website: www.pepbonet.com

Donna DeCesare
For two decades, Donna DeCesare has photographed children affected by war and gang violence, including street children. For the last seven years she has focused on children whose exposure to violence or HIV/AIDS carries the risk of social stigma. In 2007 Donna established with UNICEF a collaborative image-making process that protects the identities of children at risk and empowers them to tell their stories, while remaining visually powerful.

Donna works as a freelance photographer and videographer, teaching documentary photography and video at the University of Texas since 2002 (see www.journalism.utexas.edu/faculty/decesarebio.html). Her photographs have been published and exhibited widely, winning several prizes and earning top awards for her work for the Crimes of War website and on U.S. and Latin American gang violence.

Until May 2008, a collection of Donna's photos will be on exhibition at The Open Society Institute in Washington as Sharing Secrets: Children's Portraits' Exposing Stigma. (see www.soros.org/initiatives/photography/focus_areas/mw/12/decesare_bio)

Web: www.donnadecesare.com

Robin Hammond
Born in Wellington, New Zealand, Robin Hammond graduated in 2000 with a Diploma in Advanced Photography. Robin moved to London in 2001 for a career in photojournalism. Instead he found himself in a picture agency sorting negatives for a year before becoming a staff photographer with a photo agency. After 18 months he started his own business (www.iconphotomedia.com). Since 2004 Robin has photographed for national newspapers, particularly The Observer, Guardian and Times, for magazines and corporate clients.

His belief in the power of photography to make a difference to the lives of the under- or misrepresented led to his work with street children. Commissioned by Casa Alianza to photograph in Mexico and by Railway Children to photograph in India, Kenya, Tanzania and Russia, Robin has also worked with ChildHope on photo stories of street children in Ethiopia, with My Life in South Africa and most recently with Street Child Africa in Zimbabwe.

Marcus Lyon
Marcus is a UK-based photographer, Ambassador for Photovoice (www.photovoice.org), Director of Digital Links International (www.digital-links.org) and Chairman of the International Children's Trust (www.ictinfo.org.uk). He has won numerous awards for his work including the B&H Gold Award, Agfa Picture of the Year, D&AD Silver nomination and AOP Editorial. His images and books are held in both private and international collections including the Art Institute of Chicago and the Arts Council of Great Britain.

After reading Politics at Leeds University, Marcus worked for Amnesty International in Guatemala. This led to numerous reportage projects over the last 15 years on street children and child labour in Latin America, Africa and Asia with the JUCONI Foundations and the International Children's Trust. He has also spent considerable time documenting Paralympic sport. All Marcus' reportage work is undertaken on a pro bono basis.

Website: www.marcuslyon.com

Dario Mitidieri

Born in Villa d'Agri, Italy, Dario Mitidieri began working as a photographer for The Independent Magazine and The Sunday Telegraph in the late 1980s. In 1989 he won Press Photographer of the Year at the British Press Awards for his coverage of the massacre at China's Tiananmen Square. After winning the W. Eugene Smith Award in Humanistic Photography, Dario spent 1992 in Bombay, documenting the lives of street children. That project received many awards including European Publishers Award for Photography and the Visa d'Or.

Other awards include: Nikon Photo Essay of the Year; World Press Photo 2004, General News Stories; and Getty Images Grant in Editorial Photography. Dario has published 3 books, including Children of Bombay (published in six languages) and is a regular contributor to collective photography books.

Living in London and represented by Getty Images worldwide, Dario keeps human rights issues as a core theme of his work

59d Caversham Road; London, NW5 2DR; 020 79164062; dario@mitidieri.com
Website: www.mitidieri.com

Karen Robinson

Karen is a freelance photographer and member of Panos Pictures. Her portraits and reportage have been widely published in newspapers and magazines including The Observer, Guardian Weekend, Independent, Times, Vogue, Marie Claire, Stern, Der Spiegel and Greenpeace International.

Her interest in environmental and social issues led to reportage on displacement of the Adivasi people by India's Narmada Dam project, global warming in Alaska, child labour in India's cotton industry, and sex-trafficked women in the UK and Lithuania.

Karen's exhibitions include: 'Slave Britain, images of sex-trafficked women', by Amnesty International, Anti-Slavery International, UNICEF and Panos in St. Paul's Cathedral, London (2007); 'All Dressed Up' about young women in East Durham's former mining communities, in The Side Gallery, Newcastle (2005); 'Cocoa farmers in Ghana', in Oxo Gallery, London, in collaboration with the Fairtrade Foundation (2004); and Children living in the sewers in Romania, International Festival of Photography, Gijon, Spain (1998).

Website: www.karenrobinson.co.uk

Dieter Telemans

Dieter was born 1971 in Bujumbura, Burundi, where his parents worked for the Belgium foreign ministry. Leaving Africa at 18 for Belgium, Dieter found the only way he could enjoy the greyness of his new country was by walking around with his Nikon camera making photographs of it. After 6 years as a freelance photographer for Belgian newspaper De Morgen, Dieter returned to working on personal projects, going back to his African roots.

Reportage on music in Kinshasa led to a project on music around the world, culminating in the publication of 'Heart of Dance' (Ludion Press, 2003). Dieter has also focussed for many years on water issues such as the drying Aral Sea in Uzbekistan, floods in Bangladesh and drought in the Horn of Africa, culminating in a second book 'Troubled Waters' (Bai, 2007), a free educational map for secondary schools and a travelling exhibition.

Website: www.dietertelemans.com and www.troubledwaters.eu